Liberty & Mental Health

You Can't Have One Without the Other

R S Bennett

Order this book online at www.trafford.com
or email orders@trafford.com

Most Trafford titles are also available at major online book retailers.

Photography and sculpture of *The Choice Bell* by Matthew
"Timeless" Welter (http://www.timelesssculptures.com)

Printed in the United States of America.

ISBN: 978-1-4907-4924-2 (sc)
ISBN: 978-1-4907-4923-5 (hc)
ISBN: 978-1-4907-4925-9 (e)

Library of Congress Control Number: 2014919128

Trafford rev. 10/29/2014

 www.trafford.com

North America & international
toll-free: 1 888 232 4444 (USA & Canada)
fax: 812 355 4082

CONTENTS

ACKNOWLEDGMENTS

I'm grateful to the various people who have held workshops I have attended and to those who have written books, created videos, or put together instructional CDs that have helped me on my journey. Several are mentioned in the text. When I thought I had completed this book, I sent it off to Victoria Dolma, who edited my first book and had graciously agreed to edit this one. Not only did she correct my many grammatical errors, but she added a note that caused me to pause. Taking her criticism to heart allowed me to improve it greatly. I also want to thank Patty Brisbin and Lila King for the comments and suggestions they made during the early drafts, as well as the various people I bounced ideas around with. When I first saw *The Choice Bell*, a sculpture by Matthew "Timeless" Welter, I knew I wanted a picture of it on the cover. He was gracious enough to allow it. Any errors, omissions, or oversights found within these pages are entirely mine.

A NOTE FROM THE AUTHOR

The nation and the world have the opportunity to enter a new age of enlightenment, peace, and prosperity; yet fear, greed, ignorance, and intolerance threaten to throw the world into a dark age from which we may never recover. While the circumstances I encountered helped drive me to be a better person, I am dismayed and disheartened by the callous disregard for life and liberty I encountered, knowing others are being treated in a similar manner by those who have been sworn to protect the rights enumerated in the US Constitution.

I wanted to hunt down and kill the Los Angeles deputy sheriff who had twisted my arm behind my head and kept it there while I was strapped to a bed. This was done to me while I was in a coma in the jail ward of the county hospital. I had the skills needed, but I either closed my eyes or averted them when the deputy stood close enough to read his name tag. A few days later, I tried to kill myself from the pain, one arm still twisted behind my head, although I had managed to temporarily free the other. It was my first arrest. I worked for a small computer company; my father had been a highly decorated police officer who had been shot in the line of duty. I had been trained in troubleshooting and problem solving. My attorney, either through accident or design, helped to cover this up. Rejecting the extremes of murder and of ending my own life, I found myself on a journey that returned me to the thresholds of these paths as I sought deeper understanding.

This was the first of ten arrests, all on misdemeanor charges. I was also lost in the system twice, resulting in three arrests on one charge and a warrant being issued in the wrong name after a sheriff's deputy entered a wrong number into a computer. Officers also committed at least three unprovoked assaults against me, aside from the times they mistook my seizure activity as a direct assault against them, and I spent over thirty days strapped to a bed while in custody, including once when officers took turns kicking me, breaking my shoulder. Almost all these instances were denied, covered up, or excused away. Once your name is entered into the system, it is quite difficult to escape from its grasp. Various officers I have spoken to over the years have mentioned to me their perceived need to take matters into their own hands as the courts have let the people down. My attorneys were pretty much worthless in providing any assistance in helping me either prepare a defense or sue the authorities and were seemingly having a primary purpose to cover up abuses, achieve no-contest pleadings, and excuse away all wrongdoings by those in authority. The harshest times I had in jail were when charged with assaulting an officer.

Here are a few quotes from my time in Los Angeles:

> *It doesn't make any difference if you are guilty or innocent, just plead "no contest," that's the way the system works.* (Los Angeles County public defender, 1988)

> *Good morning scum-buckets. How the fuck are you doing this morning, assholes.* (Wake-up call, Los Angeles County Jail, 1988)

> *We have decided to defend the public by making sure everyone charged with a crime is found guilty of something.* (Los Angeles County public defender, 1989)

> *Oh no, we're wonderful. We don't do things like that.* (My elected California State assemblywoman, 1992)

However, beyond desperation, an oasis can be found. In 1992 I received honorable mention for a paper I wrote on how mental health courts could save communities money while providing better treatment for those with mental health issues. I also served on the committee that helped to form Nevada's first mental health court, and my book *Mental Illness: A Guide to Recovery* was favorably reviewed in Boston University's *Psychiatric Rehabilitation Journal* (vol. 28, no. 4, Spring 2005).

INTRODUCTION

*Everything can be taken from a human being but one thing:
the last of the human freedoms—to choose one's attitude in
any given set of circumstances, to choose one's own way.*[1]

The nation and the world face many challenges—terrorism,
rising sea levels, food shortages, lack of drinking water, income
disparities, a huge prison population, international tensions,
dissatisfied populations, increasing CO_2 levels, rise in religious
fundamentalism, wars, solitary confinement, apathy, pollution,
increased debt, deforestation, decreased nutritional value in
food, homelessness, earthquakes, decreased biodiversity, sexually
transmitted diseases, school shootings, forced electroshocks,
mandatory sentencing laws, drug addiction, floods, human
trafficking, insane drug laws, a dysfunctional mental health
system, world population expected to rise to between nine and
twelve billion by 2050, and a battle-locked Congress controlled
by special interests demanding increasingly authoritarian
measures for others to obey. Several Supreme Court decisions
appear to be the cause of much distrust with the justice system,
which sacrifices the public by building walls of immunity
protecting the rich and powerful from the consequences of their
actions, including giving unreasonable power to prosecutors,
causing loss of liberty to many. Then we have an executive
branch, which rewards Wall Street bankers for defrauding the
people. No wonder 26% of the US adult population is considered

by mental health authorities to be experiencing mental health problems in any given year.[2]

The situation those with mental health problems find themselves in can be considered a microcosm of larger social problems. While most complain of how little those on opposite sides of the political spectrum work together, often it is their shared view that the privileges of the rich and powerful must be preserved and enhanced while their abuses are denied, covered up, excused, and then justified, which prevents the nation from working together for greater harmony and cooperation. The main differences between Left and Right are that the left wing favors huge bureaucracies in order to compel the people to obey the rich and powerful, while the right wing promotes unethical behaviors—at least for corporations. Both put the interest of huge campaign contributors over that of the people and the nation. Washington, DC, is primarily inhabited by lawyers who are skilled in circumvention of the law[3] and who constantly find scapegoats to explain away their shortcomings—failures in policy and law.

> Over half of the US prison population is mentally ill, and people who suffer from mental illnesses are represented in the criminal justice system at rates between two and four times higher than in the general population. Given that studies find people with mental illnesses to be no more prone to violence than those without mental illnesses, the root of this overrepresentation in prison clearly lies in our mental health system's shortcomings. Instead of treating the underlying biological and environmental causes of these disorders, we are criminalizing and incarcerating the mentally ill.[4]

There are low-budget solutions to many of the challenges we face as a nation and a world.

> Numerous studies conducted in juvenile correctional institutions have reported that violence and serious

antisocial behavior have been cut in half after implementing nutrient-dense diets.[5]

But neither big money nor big government wants them. Ineffective high-cost solutions that are doomed to failure seem to be the preferred way of doing business. That way, narrowly focused experts can cry for even more money to dream up more unworkable solutions and receive huge fees to do so. This needs to change, although costs will come due.

Bureaucracies fight change. "The lag between discovering effective forms of treatment and incorporating them into routine patient care is unnecessarily long, lasting about 15 to 20 years."[6] All too often, growing the bureaucracy takes priority over solving the problems at hand.

Psychiatry needs to lose its dominant role in the field of mental health. Many within the profession immediately discard three-fourths of the medical model in the rush to put people on drugs. It has also been common to ignore studies from within the profession while discounting nearly everything that comes from other fields of study. "There is little collaboration among the disciplines on workforce development efforts, such as competency development, despite the presence of many shared competencies across professions."[7]

The medical model, however, is not the only model available. Ayurveda is the main system of healing in India. It is as much a way of life as a system of medicine, and it encompasses science, religion, and philosophy. Having proven effective, portions of traditional Chinese medicine are now being used in the US military and are used by a few in the treatment of those with mental health issues. The emerging field of *vibrational medicine* offers additional insight to the cause of at least one common symptom, hearing voices, as well as innovative treatment options. Additionally, while politicians, salesmen, and even some psychologists in America appear to consider being sexy, smooth talking, and insincere as desirable characteristics, Buddhist psychology considers these combined traits to be a form of neurotic behavior.

United by the belief that the rich should rule, Democrats and Republicans for decades have been transferring wealth and power from the people to Wall Street and the bureaucracies. Wall Street, of course, follows the long tradition of bankers everywhere, creating confusion and chaos in order to take advantage of the crises they help to create. Meanwhile, environmentalists wonder how a Congress controlled by Wall Street intends to bribe or otherwise pay off an ocean that is increasing in temperature and volume. Neither ruled, frightened, nor impressed by money, the forces of nature will not bend to the highest bidder. Our laws and bureaucratic priorities are driving people crazy.

Vote for us and spend the next
4 years kissing the buttocks
of the Lobbyists who own us

2013 R.S. Bennett The right to freely duplicate this image is hereby granted.

[1]   Viktor Frankl, *Man's Search for Meaning* 1946, 2006

[2]   http://www.nimh.nih.gov/health/publications/the-numbers-count-mental-disorders-in-america/index.shtml, Kessler R. C., Chiu W. T., Demler O., Walters E. E. Prevalence, severity, and comorbidity of twelve-month DSM-IV disorders in the National Comorbidity Survey Replication (NCS-R). *Archives of General Psychiatry*, 2005 Jun 62(6):617–27.

[3]   lawyer: one skilled in circumvention of the law. *The Devil's Dictionary*, by Ambrose Bierce 1911 Neale Publishing Company, 2003 The Folio Society

[4]   Why Addressing Mental Health Issues Means Reforming The US Prison System By *Rachel Howard* on Feb 8, 2013 http://thinkprogress. org/health/2013/02/08/1561341/mental-health-prison-reform/

[5]   Transdermal Magnesium Therapy 2007 by Mark Sircus, Ac., OMD, p. 173

[6]   Achieving the Promise: Transforming Mental Health Care in America; Executive Summary, Final Report July 2003(p. 2), Balas, E. A. and Boren, S. A. (2000). Managing clinical knowledge for health care improvement. In *Yearbook of Medical Information* (pp. 65–70). Bethesda, MD: National Library of Medicine.

[7]   AN ACTION PLAN ON BEHAVIORAL HEALTH WORKFORCE DEVELOPMENT by The Annapolis Coalition on the Behavioral Health Workforce 2007, p. 12

CHAPTER 1

26% OF THE US POPULATION IS EXPERIENCING MENTAL HEALTH PROBLEMS?

The Holy Inquisition was regarded as we today regard the practice of psychiatry. A heretic was a very sick man. He was much to be pitied because he held a false view he was doomed to suffer forever in the most exquisite torture chamber ever imagined. Think of entertaining that idea as seriously as we regard . . . schizophrenia today. We feel that in curing a person of disease almost anything is justified: . . . people undergoing shock treatment; people locked in the colorless, monotonous corridors of mental institutions not knowing if they will ever get out because they cannot understand what is expected of them, and the psychiatrists do not know either. It is kind of Kafka-like nightmare. We think these . . . psychiatrists are very good people, that they are righteous men working to alleviate human suffering. Well, they thought exactly the same thing about the Inquisitors. In all good faith, they knew that witchcraft and heresy were terrible things, awful plagues imperiling people's souls forever. Any means were justified to cure people of heresy; and we have not changed. We are doing the same thing today but under different names. We can look back and see how evil that was, but we cannot see it in ourselves.[8]

When reforms are needed, the phrase "There is no reason to reinvent the wheel" is often given to prevent reforms and maintain the status quo. While the wheel does not need to be reinvented, periodic maintenance, including checking the alignment, rebalancing the wheels, and checking the pressure and wear on the tires to see if they need replacement, is required. This needs to be done in the mental health system as soon as possible, preferably today.

Drugs have played an important role for many who have received a mental health diagnosis, but most of the scientific advancements made outside the field of pharmaceuticals have largely been overlooked, ignored, or dismissed by many in the forefront of the mental health system, causing needless suffering by many. Recovery from *mental illness* should and can be the norm while the prevention of the various *mental illnesses* is within reach, but it cannot and will not happen as long as drugs are the primary—and often the only—option considered.

Mental Disorders Are Common

> *Mental disorders are common in the United States and internationally. An estimated 26.2 percent of Americans ages 18 and older—about one in four adults—suffer from a diagnosable mental disorder in a given year.*[9]

> *When applied to the 2004 US Census residential population estimate for ages 18 and older, this figure translates to 57.7 million people.*[10]

> *Even though mental disorders are widespread in the population, the main burden of illness is concentrated in a much smaller proportion—about 6 percent, or 1 in 17—who suffer from a serious mental illness. In addition, mental disorders are the leading cause of disability in the US and Canada. Many people suffer from more than one*

mental disorder at a given time. Nearly half (45 percent) of those with any mental disorder meet criteria for 2 or more disorders, with severity strongly related to comorbidity.[11]

We are at a crossroads: One path leads to greater cooperation and harmony among the peoples not just of this nation but of the world. The other path leads to greater conflicts and disharmony with individuals, nations, religions, and corporate entities insisting they are superior to all others and therefore have the right to impose their will on all others.

There has been much research in various scientific fields regarding mental health. While there are differences in approach and perspective, nearly all agree that it is a combination of factors that produces good mental health.

> *Psychology originally focused on the ego and unconsciousness as the source of anxiety and stress, which meant that anxiety and stress were considered a product of social conditioning. On the other hand, neurologists have followed a trail that leads to the interaction of certain parts of the brain as a source of the emotions, while physiologists focused on the role of the nervous system in stress and anxiety. Yet another group of researchers—psychobiologists—focused on the neuropeptides and other chemicals generated in the brain and transmitted throughout the body as a major contributor to stress and anxiety . . . it's becoming increasingly clear that these different routes of research into how we experience stress, anxiety, and trauma are leading us to the recognition that body and mind are intricately linked.*[12]

Overlooked Medical Ailments in Psychiatric Populations

The *Diagnostic and Statistical Manual of Mental Disorders*, fourth edition (*DSM-IV*), cautions against using the manual in a cookbook fashion,[13] yet many in the field of mental health use it exactly that way. The problem of overlooked medical ailments in psychiatric populations was so significant that by 1988 the California legislature mandated an exploration into a means of reducing the risk of missed medical conditions. Lorrin Koran, MD, of Stanford University was tasked with leading the development of a corrective procedure. The results of his team's work were reported to the California Department of Mental Health and local mental health programs in 1991 as the *Medical Evaluation Field Manual.*[14]

> *The mental health system had detected 58 percent of test-group patients with a disease at a cost of $230 per patient. Many mental health programs are not staffed with physicians practiced in medical diagnosis and thus are unprepared to detect a large proportion of physical diseases in their patients. As described elsewhere, California's state mental health programs fail to detect many diseases that could be causing or exacerbating psychiatric disorders.*[15]

If California fails to find many diseases that cause or exacerbate psychiatric disorders, it's a good bet that every state has people who are homeless, in jail, in prison, or in extreme poverty due to lack of proper diagnosis.

The Koran Algorithm

The Koran screening algorithm[16] has several appealing characteristics:

1. It is limited to those findings that best predict the presence of physical disease in a sample of patients cared for within the California public mental health system.

2. It saves the effort and expense of gathering data that may not help in detecting physical disease.
3. The data used in the algorithm can be obtained by mental health staff and do not require a physician, nurse, or physician assistant.

The Koran medical algorithm requires ten items of medical history, measurement of blood pressure, and sixteen laboratory tests (thirteen blood tests and three urine tests). These data were the only strong predictors of physical disease in the Koran patients.

In 1995 a study found that from 5–40% of psychiatric patients have medical ailments that would adequately explain their symptoms.[17] The next year, in 1996, Sydney Walker III, MD, a psychiatrist, in his book *A Dose of Sanity*, claimed studies have shown that from 41% to 75% of individuals are initially misdiagnosed, often due to overlooked treatable conditions.[18] In 2009, it was found that up to 25% of mental health patients have medical conditions that exacerbate psychiatric symptoms.[19] Yet most of the debate today centers on forcing drugs on individuals, not providing adequate diagnosis and effective treatment.

Walker points out that the *DSM* has encouraged practitioners to label patients quickly rather than pursue the more time-consuming deductive work of differential diagnosis.[20] According to Walker, labeling leads to fitting patients into groups rather than treating them as the individuals they are, carefully taking medical histories, and performing physical examinations— all of which being absolute requirements for a valid diagnosis. Walker presents many appalling examples of patients who were routinely assigned *DSM* labels that then became masks for such often dangerous physical diseases as bowel blockage, lupus, brain tumors, and Tourette's and Klinefelter's syndromes. Walker stresses that many of the masked diseases are treatable if caught early and that many of the drugs psychiatrists prescribe are dangerous or addictive.

Ruling out the various physical ailments that can cause or exacerbate psychiatric disorders needs to be done prior to labeling a person as *mentally ill*. This label negatively impacts individuals for decades after he or she has made a complete recovery—even if the label was applied erroneously.

Recommendation

The Koran algorithm should be used regularly at emergency rooms when people are brought in for evaluations, as well as before anyone is committed to a psychiatric hospital or is sent to prison. Ideally the Koran algorithm should be performed by general practitioners every three to five years, beginning around puberty and continuing to middle age, when the onset of mental health problems begins to wane. Perhaps it should again be periodically performed when individuals enter their senior years.

According to the International Classification of Functioning, Disability, and Health (ICF), the medical model views disability as a problem of the person directly caused by disease, trauma, or other health condition that requires medical care provided in the form of individual treatment by professionals. Management of the disability is aimed at cure or the individual's adjustment and behavior change. The social model of disability sees the issue mainly as a socially created problem and a matter related to the full integration of individuals into society.

> *According to the social model, disability is not an attribute of the individual, but rather a complex collection of conditions, many of which are created by the social environment: the approach to disability requires social action and is a responsibility of society.*[21]

The National Institutes of Health in May 2013 declared the methods of American psychiatry as "lacking in validity" and stated that "patients deserve better."[22] Their key criticism was they have no objective test showing that their diagnoses are right. While a growing number of psychologists and psychiatrists decry the actions and even the motives of many within the APA, a large percentage of psychiatrists, in less than fifteen or often less than five minutes of speaking to an individual, prescribe powerful mind-altering drugs to those who have come to them for help. Patients do deserve better.

Currently, the diagnosis of mental disorders is based on clinical observation—identifying symptoms that tend to cluster together, determining when the symptoms appear, and determining whether the symptoms resolve, recur, or become chronic. However, the way that mental disorders are defined in the present diagnostic system does not incorporate current information from integrative neuroscience research, and thus is not optimal for making scientific gains through neuroscience approaches.[23]

Trauma as a Factor in Mental Health Diagnoses

Trauma is a factor for the overwhelming numbers of people who have received a mental health diagnosis. "Trauma exposure has been linked to later substance abuse, mental illness, increased risk of suicide, obesity, heart disease, and early death."[24] Unfortunately, the silo mentality[25] that has developed in the mental health system has worked to prevent the various nondrug trauma treatments from being more well-known.

The research into trauma can be quite enlightening for anyone interested in reducing the number of individuals with mental health diagnoses, using illegal drugs, committing suicide, or having other health problems, yet the APA ignored trauma symptoms except in the section on posttraumatic stress disorder

(PTSD) in the 2013 release of the *DSM-V*. The various symptoms of trauma nearly mimic all the diagnoses in the *DSM* series with variations often easily explained by individual stress responses and personality type.

> *When a traumatic event occurs, the individual feels overwhelmed and the experience seems unbearable. However it is precisely because of this overwhelming experience that the individual is forced out of their old way of thinking into a new way of being in the universe. Mahatma Gandhi, Nelson Mandela, Martin Luther King, Mother Theresa, all experienced trauma and used their painful encounters to develop a more moral and ethical response to their traumatic circumstances. Their lives demonstrate to us that the trauma recovery process contains the possibility of helping the human person develop into a more moral and ethical species. If we can repeat this process for thousands or millions of people, we can use the transforming power inherent in the trauma recovery process to transform the ethical and moral foundations of the human person.*[26]

Several proven nondrug methodologies are available to treat trauma, including Somatic Experiencing (SE), Eye Movement Desensitization and Reprocessing (EMDR), and Tension and Trauma Releasing Exercises (TRE) developed by David Berceli, PhD.

The Wellness Recovery Action Plan (WRAP),[27] devised by Mary Ellen Copeland is recognized by the Substance Abuse Mental Health Services Administration (SAMHSA) as an evidence-based practice, yet few outside the peer networks know much about it. In my opinion, WRAP is especially helpful when a trauma occurred at a young age, yet its primary focus is helping individuals plan for their recovery, including the reduction of symptoms.

At least 75% of children in the juvenile justice system have experienced traumatic victimization. As many as 50% of these youth may have symptoms of Post-Traumatic Stress Disorder. 93% of children in detention report exposure to adverse events. These adverse and potentially traumatic events include accidents and serious illnesses, physical abuse, sexual abuse, neglect, traumatic loss, domestic and community violence, growing up in a household with an alcohol or drug abuser, an incarcerated household member, someone who is chronically depressed, suicidal, institutionalized or mentally ill . . . Exposure to these adverse experiences increases a youth's risk for: Major Mental Illness; Substance Abuse; AIDS and Sexually Transmitted Diseases; Impaired Physical Health; Academic Difficulties; Early Death.[28]

Trauma can result in shrinkage of the hippocampus which is adjacent to the amygdala, and can be considered the emotional center of the brain. This shrinkage affects the communication between areas of the brain and is responsible for heightened fear and anger responses.[29] For this reason it is recommended that individuals who have experienced significant trauma take courses on managing anger. (Chapter 2 contains information on Transforming Anger.)

Most would agree that war, rape, betrayal or abandonment during childhood, severe emotional, physical, or sexual abuse—neglect, or catastrophic injury and illness can cause trauma. But were you aware that less obvious incidents, such as minor auto accidents, invasive medical and dental procedures, falls, minor injuries, natural disasters, illness, young children who are left alone, prolonged immobilization, exposure to extreme heat or cold, sudden loud noises, and even the stress of birth to both infant and mother can cause trauma?

According to *Healing Trauma*, by Peter Levine, PhD, all of the above can be causes of trauma. Dr. Levine relates in his book how he became interested in trauma. A man had gone into a convenience store at 6:30 in the morning on July 5th, and held it up for a few dollars, showing only a protrusion from his jacket pocket where his hand was. He then went to his car and waited for the police who arrested him without any resistance. As they were booking him, they noticed he was a Vietnam vet, and had been arrested several times before, every time on July 5th at 6:30 in the morning, and every time he had waited in his car for the police to show up. He was sent to a mental health facility where it was discovered that on July 4th, his entire squad had been killed except for himself and one other, who had been severely wounded. It was at 6:30 the morning of the 5th when a rescue helicopter showed up. About the same time, his buddy also died.

> *A compulsion can develop to repeat the actions that caused the problem in the first place. We are inextricably drawn into situations that replicate the original trauma in both obvious and less obvious ways . . . We may find ourselves re-experiencing the effects of trauma either through physical symptoms or through a full-blown interaction with the external environment . . . . Once he became aware of his feelings and the role the original event had played in driving his compulsion, the man was able to stop re-enacting this tragic incident.*[30]

Some symptoms of trauma arise can arise immediately, such as feelings of helplessness, immobility, and freezing, as well as an increased heart rate, sweating, difficulty breathing, cold sweats, tingling, and muscular tension, increased repetitious thoughts, racing mind, worry, constrictions in the body, a narrowing of perceptions, and dissociation and denial. Other symptoms can arise fairly soon afterward, such as hypervigilance, intrusive imagery or flashbacks, extreme sensitivity to light and sound, hyperactivity, exaggerated emotional and startle response, nightmares and night terrors, abrupt mood swings, shame and lack of self-worth, reduced ability to deal with stress, and difficulty sleeping.

If the trauma isn't successfully healed, more symptoms can appear later, such as panic attacks, anxiety, phobias, mental "blankness" or spaced-out feelings, avoidance behaviors, attraction to dangerous situations, addictive behaviors, exaggerated or diminished sexual behaviors, amnesia or forgetfulness, fear of dying or having a shortened life, self-mutilation, loss of sustaining beliefs, or inability to love, nurture, or bond.

Still other symptoms of trauma can occur years after the original trauma. These can include excessive shyness, diminished emotional responses, inability to make commitments, chronic fatigue or very low energy, immune system problems, psychosomatic illnesses, chronic pain, fibromyalgia, asthma, skin disorders, digestive problems, severe PMS, depression, feelings of impending doom, feelings of detachment, alienation, isolation, and reduced ability to formulate plans.

Recommendation

Trauma screening should be part of every mental health examination and be included in annual checkups done by general practitioners. This way, patients can be referred to one or more of the proven nondrug therapies and avoid being labeled as mentally ill, which can condemn an individual to a substandard life.

> *The symptoms of trauma can be stable, that is, ever-present. They can also be unstable, meaning they can come and go and be triggered by stress. Or they can remain hidden for decades and suddenly surface. Usually, symptoms do not occur individually, but come in groups. They often grow increasingly complex over time, becoming less and less connected with the original trauma experience.*[31]

A large portion of our nation's drug and mental health problems essentially arise from a combination of traumatized individuals and our drug policies that provide huge incentives for people to sell them on the black market.

> *Once a trauma befalls us we are forced . . . to follow its life-altering path. At times, this process often leads us through episodes of helplessness and hopelessness. It can terrify us by unveiling the fragility, precariousness and vulnerability of our humanity. It exposes us to the rawness of life as a living species on this planet. It tears at the very fabric of our identity and radically redefines our view of life. However, it is precisely because this experience has burned the bridges of our past ways of thinking that we are forced into a new way of being in life. The old ways of thinking and relating no longer suffice and a new way of being begins to emerge. We discover that on the other side of this frightening journey we have the potential of emerging into a new life of maturity, compassion and wisdom.*[32]

False Advertising by the Drug Industry

Neurotransmitter deregulation, most often called a chemical imbalance, has been touted by the various drug companies as the sole cause of the various mental illnesses. This is blatantly false. At best, these chemical imbalances are merely the result of other forces acting upon the body, including the brain. While the existence of various neurotransmitters, receptors, and chemical messengers is not being disputed here, the symptoms that can result in a mental health diagnosis can arise from many diverse causes. No *normal* amount of any of the various chemical messengers has ever been established and likely never will. Varying circumstances and environments will alter preferred ratios of chemical messengers. Normal is a variable, not an absolute.[33]

The Medical Model's Four Reasons for Brain Dysfunction

According to the biomedical model, there are four reasons for brain dysfunction:[34]

1. Anatomical abnormalities or damage
2. Lack of oxygen or glucose
3. Electrolyte imbalance
4. Neurotransmitter deregulation: the imbalance of brain chemistry

The first three of these have often been overlooked by a great many in the mental health field. In order that individuals obtain the best chance of recovery, health problems must be identified before they become major. Protocols for effective screening of mental health issues need to be incorporated into the mental health system, as well as researches from other fields that affect a person's mental health. Each of these can be a causative factor in brain dysfunction, including the so-called mental illnesses.

> *Certain drugs, such as opioids (narcotics), some sedatives (such as benzodiazepines and barbiturates), and antidepressants cause diffuse brain dysfunction if people are sensitive to their effects (as older people are) or if the level of drug in the blood is too high.*[35]

Anatomical Abnormalities or Damage:

As trauma can result in shrinkage of the hippocampus and this shrinkage affects the communication between areas of the brain, the effects of trauma should be considered as anatomical abnormalities or damage.

Korean scientists found that eight- to eleven-year-old children who had higher levels of breakdown products of one type of phthalate (DEHP) in their urine were more likely to demonstrate inattentive and hyperactive behavior. Additionally, higher levels of the breakdown product of a different type of phthalate (DBP) were associated with inattentive and impulsive performance on a standardized behavioral test. Phthalates are a class of chemicals best known for their roles in keeping plastics soft and liquids mixed. Phthalates are very common in consumer products and may be found in perfumes and other personal care products, medications, food packaging, medical devices, and vinyls.[36]

> *Neurodevelopmental disabilities, including autism, attention-deficit hyperactivity disorder, dyslexia, and other cognitive impairment, affect millions of children worldwide, and some diagnoses seem to be increasing in frequency. Industrial chemicals that injure the developing brain are among the known causes for this rise in prevalence. In 2006 . . . a systemic review . . . identified five industrial chemicals as developmental neurotoxicants: lead, methylmercury, polychlorinated biphenyls, arsenic, and toluene. Since 2006, epidemiological studies have documented six additional developmental neurotoxicants—manganese, fluoride, chlorpyrifos, dichlorodiphenyltrichloroethane, tetrachloroethylene, and the polybrominated diphenyl ethers. . . . To control the pandemic of developmental neurotoxicity, we propose a global prevention strategy. Untested chemicals should not be presumed to be safe to brain development, and chemicals in existing use and all new chemicals must therefore be tested for developmental neurotoxicity.[37]*

Psychiatric disorders after traumatic brain injury (TBI) are frequent. Research in this area is important for patients' care and may provide hints for the comprehension of primary psychiatric disorders.

> *A TBI can be penetrating or closed, depending on if there was brain tissue exposition or not. The central nervous system injuries can be primary or secondary. Primary injuries are related to the tissue impairment which results directly from the impact forces. These injuries can be localized, such as a laceration of the brain parenchyma, or diffuse lesions, as in the diffuse axonal injury. The secondary injuries are developed subsequently as tissue response to the primary injuries or to systemic events. Examples of secondary injuries are inflammation, ischemia, lack of blood flow auto regulation, and glial proliferation . . . Common sense indicates that early identification and intervention on emotional and behavioral disturbances may also improve the life quality of these patients.*[38]

Lack of Oxygen or Glucose

Lack of oxygen to the brain can cause cerebral hypoxia. As brain cells are highly sensitive to hypoxia, they quickly begin to die when they are deprived of oxygen. Stroke, carbon monoxide poisoning, heart dysfunction, drowning, and injuries sustained at birth can all cause hypoxia, which can impair brain function, cause brain damage, and lead to death. Symptoms of mild cerebral hypoxia include inattentiveness, poor judgment, memory loss, and a decrease in motor coordination.[39]

> *An intimate link exists between the brain and the metabolism of sugar—one that has too long been overlooked by the fields of neuroscience and psychiatry*

. . . insulin appears to be important in the development of several neuropsychiatric disorders, including neurodegenerative diseases such as Alzheimer's . . . an essential step in the development of preventive treatments, and targeting insulin-related pathways in the brain could lead to new approaches for treating neurological and psychiatric disorders.[40]

The thyroid is involved in the regulation of glucose. A poorly functioning thyroid is one of several often overlooked conditions in psychiatry. Psychiatric symptoms of hyperthyroidism include generalized anxiety, depression, irritability, hypomania, cognitive dysfunction, and mania (in severe hyperthyroidism—thyrotoxicosis, or thyroid storm). Psychiatric symptoms of hypothyroidism include depression, cognitive dysfunction, psychosis (in severe hypothyroidism—myxedema madness). Other psychiatric symptoms include depression, rapid cycling in bipolar disorder (a common cause), and subtle signs of cognitive dysfunction.[41]

Another generally ignored area is the adrenal glands, which "work with the pancreas to balance blood sugar levels and also create cortisol, which has many functions, including to help increase blood sugar levels and make the cells more receptive to thyroid hormones. Weakened adrenals and low cortisol can result in nervousness, anxiety, racing heart, nausea, hot flashes, dizziness, and shakiness. The pituitary gland produces the human growth hormone as well as hormones for the thyroid, adrenals, kidneys, and both male and female sex organs."[42]

Electrolyte Imbalance

Magnesium, sodium, chloride, potassium, and calcium are known as electrolytes, minerals that dissolve in water and form electrically charged particles called ions. These ions are essential for transmitting electrical impulses along nerves and for muscle contraction. They create electrical impulses that let cells in our body send messages back and forth to one another (cell communication) and through this allow individuals to perform the *bioelectrical* functions, such as thinking, moving, and seeing.

Electrolyte deficiencies, especially of magnesium, due to the decreased nutritional value of the food we now eat, may be one of the major reasons so many people are being diagnosed with mental health problems.

> *Magnesium deficiency causes serotonin-deficiency with possible resultant aberrant behaviors, including depression, suicide or irrational violence.*[43]

In 1936, testimony was put before the American Congress attesting that the food we produce and eat was devoid of basic nutrients. Over 70 years later, the situation is far worse and the basic picture is frightening. . . . No man, woman or child today can eat enough fruits and vegetables to supply their bodies with enough magnesium for perfect health. There has been a gradual decline of dietary magnesium . . . from a high of 500mg/day at the turn of the last century to barely 175–225 mg/day today.[44]

Magnesium (Mg^{2+}) works with copper and calcium to increase bone health. It also allows the body to utilize vitamin C, vitamin B$_1$, choline, and biotin. It is an essential component of some enzymes, including those that break down carbohydrates and cholesterol, and necessary for a healthy reproductive system. It's thought to help stimulate connective tissue growth and brain development and neutralize free radicals. Insufficient amounts of magnesium in the body can lead to muscle pain, insomnia, migraines, menstrual pain, heart failure, and depression.

The immune response, nerve and brain function, blood pressure, and over three hundred enzymatic reactions rely on magnesium. Magnesium toxicity is generally related to severe renal insufficiency where the kidneys lose the ability to remove any excess.

> *Magnesium is essential in regulating central nervous system excitability thus magnesium deficiency may cause aggressive behavior, depression, or suicide. Magnesium calms the brain and people do not need to become severely deficient in magnesium for the brain to become hyperactive . . . a marginal magnesium intake overexcites the brain's neurons and results in less coherence—creating cacophony rather than symphony—according to electroencephalogram (EEG) measurements.*[45]

> *Evidence is mounting that deficient levels of magnesium contribute to the heavy metal deposition in the brain that precede Parkinson's disease, multiple sclerosis and Alzheimer's disease. . . . Another study found that the lower the magnesium blood levels the more severe was the epilepsy.*[46]

Recommendation

Checking magnesium levels should become routine in the mental health system and in prisons and youth correctional facilities. Ideally they should also be done by general practitioners.

Sodium (Na$^+$) is essential for maintaining blood pressure and helps ensure proper function of nerves and proper muscle function. It also helps in digestion and bone formation and keeps the body from becoming too acidic or too alkaline. When sodium levels are high, the body retains more water, raising blood pressure (hypertension), as increased water makes the heart work harder. Too little sodium can result in muscle cramps, muscle weakness, headache, nausea, and fatigue.

Table salt is a form of sodium chloride derived from various sources, including salt from the sea. The refining process typically removes trace minerals and adds chemicals, sugar, and iodine. Unrefined salt retains naturally occurring trace minerals like magnesium, potassium, iron, and calcium, which means that it has lower sodium content. These trace minerals also make unrefined salt more nutritious. Salt used in processed foods is typically refined but not iodized. Iodine is added to most table salt as too little iodine can result in goiter due to thyroid enlargement and also impairs fetal brain development. Salt alternatives include sage, thyme, cumin, rosemary, and basil. Seaweeds, typically various types of kelp, including dulse, alaria, and laver, are favorites among many Asians.

Chloride (Cl⁻) is a crucial part of hydrochloric acid needed by the stomach to break down food. It is also needed for the liver to function properly and for healthy joints. Like sodium, it prevents the body from becoming too acidic or too alkaline. A typical normal range is 96–106 milliequivalents per liter (mEq/L). A greater-than-normal level of chloride is called hyperchloremia. It may be due to bromide poisoning, carbonic anhydrase inhibitors (used to treat glaucoma), diarrhea, metabolic acidosis, respiratory alkalosis, or renal tubular acidosis. A lower-than-normal level of chloride is called hypochloremia. It may be due to Addison's disease, Bartter syndrome, burns, congestive heart failure, dehydration, excessive sweating, gastric suction, hyperaldosteronism, metabolic alkalosis, or respiratory acidosis.[47]

Potassium (K⁺) helps to maintain blood pressure and is needed for muscle contraction and nerve impulse transmission. It also aids digestion. There is no specific RDA for potassium, though it is believed at least 2–2.5 grams per day are needed, or about 0.8–1.5 grams per 1,000 calories consumed. For hyperkalemia, or elevated potassium levels, to occur, usually other factors are involved; decrease in renal function is the most likely cause. Major infection, gastrointestinal bleeding, and rapid protein breakdown may also cause elevated potassium levels. Cardiac function can be affected by hyperkalemia.

Deficiency of potassium is more common, especially with aging or chronic disease. Fatigue is the most common symptom of chronic potassium deficiency. Early symptoms can include muscle weakness, slow reflexes, and dry skin or acne and can progress to nervous disorders, insomnia, slow or irregular heartbeat, and loss of gastrointestinal tone. Some common problems associated with low potassium levels include hypertension, congestive heart failure, cardiac arrhythmia, fatigue, and depression and other mood changes. A sudden loss of potassium may lead to cardiac arrhythmia. Low potassium may impair glucose metabolism and lead to elevated blood sugar. In more severe potassium deficiency, there can be serious muscle weakness, bone fragility, central nervous system changes, decreased heart rate, and even death.

Calcium (Ca^{2+}) is important for the formation of teeth and bone. Roughly 99% of the body's calcium is found in the teeth and bones. Calcium is also needed for muscles to contract properly and for blood to clot normally and is important in controlling high blood pressure.

Insufficient intakes of calcium do not produce obvious short-term symptoms because the body maintains calcium levels in the blood by taking it from bone. Over the long term, low calcium intakes have health consequences, such as low bone mass (osteopenia), which increases the risks of osteoporosis and bone fractures. Symptoms of serious calcium deficiency include numbness and tingling in the fingers, convulsions, and abnormal heart rhythms, which can lead to death. These symptoms occur almost always in people with serious health problems or who are undergoing certain medical treatments. Getting too much calcium can cause constipation. While not well established, it may interfere with the body's ability to absorb iron and zinc. In adults, too much calcium (from dietary supplements but not food) may increase the risk of kidney stones. Some studies show that people who consume high amounts of calcium have increased risks of prostate cancer and heart disease.

The medical model for brain dysfunction seems to neglect the other twelve minerals known to be necessary for human life: iodine, phosphorus, iron, sulfur, zinc, chromium, cobalt, copper, fluoride, manganese, molybdenum, and selenium, as well as other elements (e.g., boron, chromium) that are known to have a role but the exact biochemical nature is unknown and others (e.g., arsenic, silicon) that are suspected to have a role in health but without proof.

Iodine (I^-) is essential for the formation of thyroid hormones, which regulate the metabolism, growth and development, and protein synthesis to maintain healthy skin, hair, and nails. Iodine was added to most table salt as too little iodine can result in goiter due to thyroid enlargement, and iodine deficiency also impairs fetal brain development. Salt used in processed foods is typically refined but not iodized. Too much iodine may cause problems, such as acne, and too little may cause hypothyroidism and in rare cases goiter.

Phosphorus (P_4^{-3}) is required for teeth and bone formation and to make chemicals that break down carbohydrates, proteins, and fats so that energy can be released.

Iron (Fe) is needed for the transfer of oxygen between tissues in our body and is essential for a healthy immune system.

Sulfur (S) is needed for the formation of cartilage, tissue, hair, and nails and for metabolic processes and for a healthy nervous system.

Zinc (Zn) is needed for the functioning of many enzymes. It helps to boost the immune system, blood clotting, growth, and repair of tissues. It also regulates cholesterol and sugar levels in our blood and blood pressure.

Chromium (Cr) is involved in blood glucose regulation, enhancing the action of insulin, which prevents blood glucose levels from getting too high, a condition called hyperglycemia.

Cobalt (Co) is required for the formation of red blood cells and for the proper functioning of some enzymes.

Copper (Cu) acts as an antioxidant, helps with the formation of red blood cells, is a component of many enzymes, and is necessary for keeping nerves, blood vessels, immune system, and bones healthy.

Fluoride (F⁻) helps to maintain the teeth by making them stronger and preventing tooth decay and helps with new bone formation and maintaining healthy bones. New studies show that fluoride is also a neurotoxin.[48]

Manganese (Mn) is an essential component of some enzymes, including those that break down carbohydrates and cholesterol. It is also necessary for a healthy reproductive system, bone formation, and proper function of the nervous system and muscles.

Molybdenum (Mo) is an essential component of some enzymes, including those that break down proteins. It also helps with normal growth and development.

Selenium (Se) is required for healthy heart function and boosts the immune system by fighting bad bacteria and viruses. It is a powerful antioxidant associated with vitamin E activity and an essential component of some enzymes.

A Hair Tissue Mineral Analysis (HTMA) can identify various mineral deficiencies and the presence of toxic substances that can cause or contribute to symptoms generally attributed to mental illness. The United States Environmental Protection Agency published a three-hundred-page study[49] in which they reviewed over four hundred medical reports on hair testing. The authors concluded that hair is a "meaningful and representative tissue for biological monitoring for most of the toxic metals."

I'm aware of a successful businesswoman in Carson City who began acting strangely and was diagnosed with schizophrenia. At the urging of her hippie mother, a HTMA was performed and it was determined that she had high levels of arsenic in her system. After the arsenic was flushed out, her symptoms disappeared and she was able to stop medications without any difficulties. She also stopped eating vegetables she had grown in her garden, which was located on mine tailings. Arsenic is naturally occurring and was also used in the mining industry.

Brain Imaging and Other Tools

While the National Institute for Mental Health states that "adolescents with childhood onset schizophrenia show four times the normal rate of gray matter loss in the front of the brain"[50] and gives the illness as the rationale for structural changes in the brain, some claim that extended drug use, including prescription drugs, is one cause of structural changes in the brain.[51]

Positron emission tomography (PET), computed tomography (CT), single-photon emission computed tomography (SPECT), and magnetic resonance imaging (both MRI and *f*MRI (functional MRI)—the first is a snapshot of brain functioning while the second is a video) are medical imaging techniques that produce images of functional processes in the body, including those in the brain. They need to be performed to investigate if structural problems or patterning in the brain are at the root of behavioral problems. After identifying specific areas or patterns that cause of malfunctioning in the brain, due to tumors, injury, or other reasons, proper treatment may begin. Drugs can help individuals on their recovery path and should not automatically be ruled out, but they should not be considered the main treatment and should be maintained at the lowest possible level.

> *The clinical effect of chronic exposure to psychoactive substances, including psychiatric drugs, produces effects very similar to those of close-head injury due to traumatic brain injury (TBI) or the postconcussive syndrome. . . . including stimulants, benzodiazepines, lithium and antipsychotic drugs.*[52]

In the popular PBS program and in the book *Healing ADD: The Breakthrough Program that Allows You to See and Heal the 7 Types of ADD*, Dr. Daniel G. Amen, a neuropsychiatrist, talks about the seven types of attention deficit disorder (ADD) that he was able to identify by using brain scans. The seven types (classic ADD, inattentive ADD, overfocused ADD, temporal lobe ADD, limbic ADD, ring-of-fire and anxious ADD) show up differently in MRIs and he discovered that treatments, including changes in lifestyles and dietary adjustments, as well as some medications, proved to be the most effective, with different types of ADD requiring differing courses of action. It is likely similar types of brain patterns will eventually be found for most instances of mental illnesses, leading to recognition of the various possible underlying reasons for apparent brain malfunction. These various patterns of brain activity have likely always been present, but the technology to see them has only existed for the past thirty years or so. Replacing the *DSM* with sound scientific reasoning for the various difficult behaviors will allow psychiatry to earn back the trust the profession has lost over the past few decades, ending the domination by drug companies in the treatment of mental health problems.

Open Dialogue

Finland, with its Open Dialogue method of treating those with mental health problems, leads the Western world in helping individuals recover from mental illness. This approach aims to support the individual's network of family and friends and to respect the decision making of the individual.[53]

> *The 20-year results, like the 15-year results, showed that patients diagnosed with schizophrenia (and those patients with mood disorders with psychosis) who took antipsychotic medication regularly during the 20 years actually experienced more psychosis, more anxiety, and were more cognitively impaired and had fewer periods of sustained recovery than those who quit taking antipsychotic medications . . . By seven years, the discontinuation group had achieved twice the functional recovery rate: 40.4 percent vs. only 17.6 percent among the medication maintenance group.*[54]

Chiropractic Examinations

A chiropractic examination (preferably with a network spinal analysis or other soft touch method, to eliminate the dangers associated with typical chiropractic methods) can identify, diminish, or eliminate blockages in the flow of cerebrospinal fluid (CSF). This fluid circulates through the skull and spinal column, bathing the brain in needed nutrients and flushing out waste material.

> *A study published in 1975, compared chiropractic care with drug treatment in children with learning and behavioral impairments due to neurological dysfunction. It was reported that chiropractic care "was more effective for the wide range of symptoms common in the neurological dysfunction syndrome in which thirteen symptom or problem areas were considered." The author also reported that chiropractic care was 24% more effective than commonly used medications.*[55]

Political Motivations

In "Why Anti-Authoritarians are Diagnosed as Mentally Ill," Bruce Levine, PhD, makes the case that anti-authoritarians are more likely to receive a mental health diagnosis than the general population and that the majority of professionals who diagnose them are authoritarians.

> *Anti-authoritarians question whether an authority is a legitimate one before taking that authority seriously. Evaluating the legitimacy of authorities includes assessing whether or not authorities actually know what they are talking about, are honest, and care about those people who are respecting their authority. And when anti-authoritarians assess an authority to be illegitimate,*

they challenge and resist that authority—sometimes aggressively and sometimes passive-aggressively, sometimes wisely and sometimes not.[56]

Authoritarian: characterized by or favoring absolute obedience to authority, as against individual freedom.[57]

As our bureaucracies, as well as both Republicans and Democrats in Congress, have become believers in authoritarian top-down government, political views seem to be partially responsible for the large number of people diagnosed, drugged, and imprisoned. Confounding this situation is the fact that many of the authorities cited by proponents of forced treatment, which usually means forced drugging, are considered charlatans, dupes, or con artists by others. Perhaps the kindest way to refer to most of these "experts" would be as residing in the category of Know-It-Alls in the *How To Deal With Difficult People* [58]grid, which is outlined in chapter 2, or, as Thich Nhat Hanh puts it, "Knowledge is considered an obstacle for understanding. If we take something to be the truth, we may cling to it so much that even if the truth comes and knocks at the door, we won't want to let it in."[59]

It should be noted that most, if not all, of those involved in school shootings and other acts of violence were on psychotropic drugs,[60] which act to dull the mind, limiting the options individuals can conceive. It also appears that the vast majority of individuals, including those claimed to be mentally ill people who resort to extreme acts of violence, fall within the grenade category of the personality grid, which is outlined in chapter 2.

What those in the West view as mental illness, the Dagara people regard as "good news from the other world." The person going through the crisis has been chosen as a medium for a message to the community that needs to be communicated from the spirit realm. "Mental disorder, behavioral disorder of all kinds, signal the fact that two obviously incompatible energies have merged into the same field," says Dr. Somé. These disturbances result when the person does not get assistance in dealing with the presence of the energy from the spirit realm.[61]

According to an article published by Rev. Richard York,[62] Jesus Christ was considered to be *existemi*—mentally ill—by many of his neighbors and relatives, including his mother, Mary, and gives Mark 3:19b–21, 31–35[63] as his source. Just as humans have a biofeedback mechanism they can access, the planet has one as well; various spiritual leaders around the world have been the ones able to understand the messages they received and, with varying degrees of success, been able to convey universal messages to others.

The mental health system needs maintenance, including checking the alignment, rebalancing the wheels, and checking the pressure and wear on the tires, but there are those who, while claiming to advocate for a better system, appear to be in favor of stepping backward. The Treatment Advocacy Center (TAC) and its founder, Dr. E. Fuller Torrey, have been at the forefront of this movement. Dr. Torrey earned his standing in the mental health community for proving stress is a factor in both the onset and relapse of schizophrenia, but for the past twelve to fourteen years, he has seemingly dedicated himself to increase the stress that those with mental health problems are under, and apparently he opposes all programs that help individuals stabilize themselves and deal better with the challenges they encounter. His drug-only and forced drugging program has been at least partially responsible for the huge increase in the number of people imprisoned in this nation. Dr. Torrey needs to step back and ask himself if he is doing more harm than good.

Screening to Regain Mental Health

The intent of the screening must be to increase mental health (happiness and contentment), not as most screenings currently are—which aim to isolate and demonize those who are seen as possible dangers so they can be drugged or otherwise neutralized.

Noncrisis Screening

It is important that screenings occur in a collegial, nonthreatening manner and be conducted by an individual who is sincerely seeking to help individuals make choices, which will increase his or her happiness and contentment with life. For some, this may mean asking and answering the questions themselves prior to reaching out for assistance.

A. What are your hopes and dreams?
B. What is your history of trauma?
C. Do you have any emotional problems that you are aware of?
D. Do you have difficulties recognizing or identifying the emotions you are having?
E. Do you recognize any patterns in the difficulties you have been experiencing?
F. How do you generally place yourself on the personality grid in chapter 2?
    a. Does this change when you are under stress? If so, how?
    b. Do you generally like how you are now?
    c. Would you like to be nearer the center of the grid?
    d. Do you have some need to be in the quadrant you are in now?
G. What obstacles are you currently facing?
H. Have you faced similar obstacles in the past?

a. If yes, how did you handle it then?
I. What are the things that make you angry?
   a. What do you think is the best way to handle your anger?
   b. Would you like to reduce the intensity or frequency of your anger?
J. What are your fears?
K. Is there anything going on right now that is bothering you?
L. What are the best ways you can do to improve your life?

For those in a crisis situation, the use of Emotional CPR or other de-escalation methods will need to be utilized and the individual must arrive at stability prior to the screening.

[8]   The Way of Liberation, Essays and Lectures on Transformation of the Self, by Alan Watts 1983, 2000 pp. 65–66

[9]   Prevalence, severity, and comorbidity of twelve-month DSM-IV disorders in the National Comorbidity Survey Replication (NCS-R) Kessler RC, Chiu WT, Demler O, Walters EE. . *Archives of General Psychiatry*, 2005 Jun;62(6):617–27; http://www.nimh.nih.gov/health/publications/the-numbers-count-mental-disorders-in-america/index.shtml

[10]   US Census Bureau Population Estimates by Demographic Characteristics. Table 2: Annual Estimates of the Population by Selected Age Groups and Sex for the United States: April 1, 2000 to July 1, 2004 (NC-EST2004-02) Source: Population Division, US Census Bureau Release Date: June 9, 2005. http://www.census.gov/popest/national/asrh/;

[11]   The Numbers Count Mental Disorders in America, Dec.12, 2008 National Institute of Mental Health

[12]   The Revolutionary Trauma Release Process – Transcend Your Toughest Times, by David Bercelli, PhD, 2008, p. 32

[13]   The Diagnostic and Statistical Manual of Mental Disorders, Fourth Edition (DSM-IV) 1994; p. xxiii

[14]   MEDICAL EVALUATION FIELD MANUAL By Lorrin M. Koran, MD, Department of Psychiatry and Behavioral Sciences, Stanford University Medical Center Stanford, California 1991.
(http://www.alternativementalhealth.com/articles/fieldmanual.htm)

[15]   A Medical Algorithm for Detecting Physical Disease in Psychiatric Patients, Hospital and Community Psychiatry Vol. 40 No. 12 Dec 1989, p. 1270 by Harold C. Sox, Jr., MD, Lorrin M. Koran, MD, Carol H. Sox, MS, Keith I. Marton, MD, Fred Dugger, PA, Teruko Smith, RN – The article can be found in the appendix.

[16]   MEDICAL EVALUATION FIELD MANUAL By Lorrin M. Koran, MD,

[17]   Allen MH, Fauman MA, Morin SF. Emergency psychiatric evaluation of "organic" mental disorders. New Dir Mental Health Serv 1995;67:45–55.

[18] *A Dose of Sanity* by Sydney Walker III, MD, 1996, pg 13/ Hoffman, Robert Science News, Vol. 122, September 11, 1982; Herringm M. M., *Debate over 'false positive schizophrenics' Medicine Tribune,* September 25, 1985. Pg 3; Koranyi, Erwin K., *"Undiagnosed physical illness in psychiatric patients," American Family Physician, Vol. 41, No. 4,* April 1990

[19] Christensen RC, Grace GD, Byrd JC. Refer more patients for medical evaluation. Curr Psychiatr 2009;8:73–74.

[20] *A Dose of Sanity* by Sydney Walker III, MD 1996

[21] Neurological disorders: public health challenges, World Health Organization 2006, p. 10

[22] Psychology Today, May 4, 2013 http://www.psychologytoday.com/blog/side-effects/201305/the-nimh-withdraws-support-dsm-5 also see Transforming Diagnosis *By Thomas Insel Director NIMH on April 29, 2013* which can be found in the appendix

[23] National Institute of Mental Health Strategic Plan, 2008, p. 9

[24] *Leading Change: A Plan for SAMHSA's Roles and Actions 2011–2014 – p. 8*

[25] AN ACTION PLAN ON BEHAVIORAL HEALTH WORKFORCE DEVELOPMENT by The Annapolis Coalition on the Behavioral Health Workforce 2007, p. 12

[26] David Berceli, PhD, CEO of Trauma Recovery Services, www.TREcalifornia.com

[27] See: http://copelandcenter.com/wellness-recovery-action-plan-wrap for more info on WRAP

[28] *Child Trauma and Juvenile Justice: Prevalence, Impact and Treatment, Dr. Gene Griffin, Department of Psychiatry Northwestern University's Feinberg School of Medicine in Chicago – Justice Center –The Council on State Government* www.consensusproject.org

[29] Does Stress Damage the Brain, by J. Douglas Bremmer MD, Biologivcal Psychiatry 1999; 45:797-805; Traumatic Amnesia, Repression, and Hippocampus Injury due to Emotional Stress, Cortisosteroids and Enkephalins by R. Joseph, Ph.D. Child Psychiatry Hum Dev. 1998 Winter;29(2):169-85. http://www.ncbi.nlm.nih.gov/pubmed/9816735

[30] *Healing Trauma by Peter Levine PhD, 2005, pp. 20, 22*

[31] *Healing Trauma* by Peter Levine, PhD, p. 20, 2005

[32] David Berceli, PhD, CEO of Trauma Recovery Services, www. TREcalifornia.com

[33] For more information on this subject see: Molecules of Emotions 1997 and Your Body is your Subconscious Mind 2004, both by Candice Pert, PhD, who was on the team which proved the existence of neurotransmitters.

[34] Biology and Human Behavior: The Neurological Origins of Individuality, Professor Robert Sapolsky, Stanford University, The Great Courses, The Teaching Company 1996

[35] Chronic stress predisposes brain to mental disorders Press Trust of India | Washington | Updated: Feb 13 http://www.business-standard.com/article/pti-stories/chronic-stress-predisposes-brain-to-mental-disorders-114021300989_1.html

[36] Phthalates may play a role in ADHD symptoms .http://www.environ mentalhealthnews.org/ehs/newscience/phthalates-may-have-a-role-in-adhd/

[37] Neurobehavioural effects of developmental toxicity, by Philippe Grandjean, Philip J. Landrigan, Lancet Neurol 2014; 13:330–338 Published online Feb. 15, 2014 http://dx.doi.org/10.1016/S1474-4422(13)70278-3/ http://www.thelancet.com/journals/laneur/article/PIIS1474-4422(13)70278-3/fulltext

[38] Psychiatric disorders and traumatic brain injury Marcelo Schwarzbold, Alexandre Diaz, [. . .], and Roger Walz, http://www.ncbi.nlm.nih.gov/pmc/articles/PMC2536546/

[39] What Are the Effects of Lack of Oxygen to the Brain? By Blake Biddulph http://www.ninds.nih.gov/disorders/anoxia/anoxia.htm

[40] Metabolism and the Brain - Evidence for the role of insulin in mediating normal and abnormal brain function may lead to new treatments for neurological and psychiatric disorders. By Oksana Kaidanovich-Beilin, Danielle S. Cha, and Roger S. McIntyre http://www.the-scientist.com/?articles.view/articleNo/33338/title/Metabolism-and-the-Brain/| December 1, 2012

[41] Complementary and Alternative Medicine Treatments in Psychiatry (p. 28) Levenson, JL. Psychiatric issues in endocrinology. Primary Psychiatry 2006;13:27–30. Canaris GJ, Manowitz NR, Mayor G, Ridgway EC. The Colorado thyroid disease study prevalence. Arch

Intern Med 2000;160:526–534 Cole DP, Thase ME, Mallinger AG, et al. Slower treatment response in bipolar depression predicted by lower pretreatment thyroid function. Am J Psychiatry 2002;159:116–121.

[42] Depression is not a drug deficiency, Alternatives for the health conscious individual, April 2008, Vol. 12 No. 10, Dr. David Williams; Biology and Human Behavior: The Neurological Origins of Individuality, Professor Robert Sapolsky, Stanford University, Lecture 6 Endocrinology: Generating an Endocrine Signal, The Great Courses, The Teaching Company 1996

[43] *Transdermal Magnesium Therapy* 2007 by Mark Sircus, Ac., OMD, p. 172

[44] *Transdermal Magnesium Therapy* 2007 by Mark Sircus, Ac., OMD, p. 291

[45] Transdermal Magnesium Therapy 2007 by Mark Sircus, Ac., OMD p. 5

[46] Ibid. p. 100

[47] http://www.nlm.nih.gov/medlineplus/ency/article/003485.htm

[48] Neurobehavioural effects of developmental toxicity, by Philippe Grandjean, Philip J. Landrigan, Lancet Neurol 2014; 13:330–338 Published online Feb. 15, 2014 http://dx.doi.org/10.1016/S1474-4422 (13)70278-3

[49] US Environmental Protection Agency Publication No 600/3-80-089. Washington, DC, Government Printing Office, 1980. Maugh, TH, Hair: A Diagnostic Tool to Complement Blood, Serum and Urine, Science, 2021271-1273(1978).

[50] National Institute of Mental Health Strategic Plan, 2008, pg 14; Thompson PM, Vidal C, Giedd JN, Gochman P, Blumenthal J, Nicolson R, Toga AW, Rapoport JL. Mapping adolescent brain change reveals dynamic wave of accelerated gray matter loss in very early-onset schizophrenia. *Proc Natl Acad Sci U S A.* 2001 Sep 25;98(20):11650-5.

[51] A review of *Anatomy of an Epidemic,* Magic Bullets, Psychiatric Drugs, and the Astonishing Rise of Mental Illness in America, by Robert Whitaker; New York, Crown Publishers, 2010 in Z Magazine, September 2010, By Bruce Levine.

[52] Psychiatric drug-induced Chronic Brain Impairment (CBI): Implications for longterm treatment with psychiatric medication by Peter R. Breggin International Journal of Risk and Safety in Medicine 23 (2011) 193–200 DOI 10.3233/JRS-2011-0542 IOS Press

[53] Five-year experience of first-episode nonaffective psychosis in open-dialogue approach: Treatment principles, follow-up outcomes, and two case studies - Psychotherapy Research, March 2006; 16(2): 214/228; A TWO YEAR FOLLOW-UP ON OPEN DIALOGUE TREATMENT IN FIRST EPISODE PSYCHOSIS: NEED FOR HOSPITALIZATION AND NEUROLEPTIC MEDICATION DECREASES, Jaakko Seikkula, Birgitta Alakare, Jukka Aaltonen - Published in Social and Clinical Psychiatry. 2000, 10(2), 20–29.

[54] Why Drugging All Schizophrenics For Life Is Not the Answer *September 19, 2013* AlterNet / *By Bruce E. Levin* http://www.alternet.org/why-drugging-all-schizophrenics-life-not-answer?paging=off

[55] Children, ADD/ADHD, and Chiropractic by Dr. Christopher Kent http://www.subluxation.com/children-addadhd-and-chiropractic/

[56] "Why Anti-Authoritarians are Diagnosed as Mentally Ill," Bruce Levine, PhD. http://www.madinamerica.com/2012/02/why-anti-authoritarians-are-diagnosed-as-mentally-ill/

[57] The American Heritage Dictionary of the English Language 1980 by Houghton Mifflin Company

[58] *How to Deal With Difficult People by* Dr. Rick Brinkman and Dr. Rick Kirschner, 1982

[59] *The Heart of Understanding, 1988 by Thich Nhat Hanh (p. 8)*

[60] SSRI Stories, Antidepressant Nightmares, "We Speak for the Dead to Protect the Living," http://www.ssristories.com/index.php?p=school; Prescription Drugs Associated with Reports of Violence Towards Others, http://www.ncbi.nlm.nih.gov/pmc/articles/PMC3002271/

[61] The Shamanic View of Mental Illness, http://www.jaysongaddis.com/2010/11/the-shamanic-view-of-mental-illness/ *(Excerpted from The Natural Medicine Guide to Schizophrenia, pages 178–189, or The Natural Medicine Guide to Bi-polar Disorder)*

[62] The Journal Vol. 3 No. 4, 1992 RELIGIOUS OUTREACH, Something Discarded; by Rev.Richard York

[63] *and they went into an house.[20] And the multitude cometh together again, so that they could not so much as eat bread.[21] And when his friends heard of it, they went out to lay hold on him: for they said, He is beside himself. [31]There came then his brethren and his mother, and, standing without, sent unto him, calling him. [32] And the multitude sat about him, and they said unto him, Behold, thy mother and thy brethren without seek for thee. [33] And he answered them, saying, Who is my mother, or my brethren? [34] And he looked round about on them which sat about him, and said, Behold my mother and my brethren! [35] For whosoever shall do the will of God, the same is my brother, and my sister, and mother. [Mark 3:19b–21, 31–35 – King James Version]*

CHAPTER 2

PSYCHOLOGICAL COUNSELING, TRAUMA, AND RECOVERY-CENTERED EDUCATION PROGRAMS

Counseling

> *Half of clients achieve a beneficial outcome in 5 to 10 sessions, whereas one-fifth to one-third will need more than 25 sessions to achieve a positive outcome . . . Forty percent of positive outcomes can be attributed to extra-therapeutic factors, that is, factors essentially out of the counselor's hands.*[64]

Many individuals find counseling beneficial, even when various dysfunctions have their origin in mineral deficiencies, trauma, thyroid problems, or other identifiable, treatable causes. Knowing a little about the various flavors of counseling can help individuals choose a method that is most compatible with their own belief system. If one approach is not a good fit, a different approach may be more successful.

I received thirty to forty sessions of cognitive-based group therapy. By the third or fourth session, I felt I was making progress and that continued until the sessions were forced to come to an end when the therapist left the rural area I lived in. He had agreed to come to the area for two years in exchange for his student loans being forgiven. I believe these types of programs should be encouraged. At least three extra-therapeutic factors played a part in my recovery as well. The first two were starting meditation and journaling. These began as a result of reading and doing the exercises in the book *The Artist Way* by Julia Cameron, who recommended meditation and journaling for anyone who was interested in becoming more creative. Meditation calms the mind, while journaling helps gently bring things to the conscious mind from the subconscious. The third extra-therapeutic factor was going to the local library and checking out the video series *How To Deal With Difficult People* by Dr. Rick Brinkman and Dr. Rick Kirschner. This video series helped me to understand the various personality traits I had developed during my first forty years of life. The cognitive-based therapy helped me take the steps needed to begin changing behaviors that no longer served me. Living in a rural area where I could walk into a forest in less than ten minutes also helped my state of mind.

Ten Things We Can Do to Contribute to Internal, Interpersonal, and Organizational Peace[65]

(1) Spend some time each day quietly reflecting on how we would like to relate to ourselves and others.

(2) Remember that all human beings have the same needs.

(3) Check our intentions to see if we are as interested in others getting their needs met as our own.

(4) When asking someone to do something, check first to see if we are making a request or a demand.

(5) Instead of saying what we *don't* want someone to do, say what we *do* want the person to do.

(6) Instead of saying what we want someone to *be*, say what action we'd like the person to take that we hope will help the person be that way.

(7) Before agreeing or disagreeing with anyone's opinions, try to tune in to what the person is feeling and needing.

(8) Instead of saying no, say what need of ours prevents us from saying yes.

(9) If we are feeling upset, think about what need of ours is not being met and what we could do to meet it, instead of thinking about what's wrong with others or ourselves.

(10) Instead of praising someone who did something we like, express our gratitude by telling the person what need of ours that action met.

The Center for Nonviolent Communication (CNVC) would like there to be a critical mass of people using Nonviolent Communication language so all people will get their needs met and resolve their conflicts peacefully.

Despite various perspectives, at one time psychiatrists generally believed something along the line of what M. Scott Peck wrote in *The Road Less Traveled*: "This tendency to avoid problems and the emotional suffering inherent in them is the primary basis of all human mental illness. Since most of have this tendency to a greater or lesser degree, most of us are mentally ill to a greater or lesser degree, lacking complete mental health."[66] This is no longer true. Currently, it appears that the majority of psychiatrists are primarily concerned with drugging individuals so they are unable to deal with the difficulties they face. Psychiatry has largely abandoned its *raison d'etre*. Perhaps this is due to psychiatrists who haven't been able to adequately face their own emotional problems, not to mention the larger social problems we all face.

Types of Counseling

Classical Psychoanalysis: Developed by Sigmund Freud, the primary techniques of classical psychoanalysis are free association and interpretation. Unresolved conflicts are frequently revisited with the expectation that transference offers the best opportunity for healing. It is often criticized for being culture-bound and chauvinistic, for reducing religion to having a psychological basis, and for failures of the client to agree with the analyst's interpretation, often being attributed to repression on the client's part. Therapy can be quite expensive, lasting for years, with sessions held several times a week. Psychoanalysis is not on the list of APA's empirically supported approaches to psychotherapy.

More information about psychoanalysis can be found at the APA's website: http://www.apa.org/.

Self-Psychology: This was developed by Heinz Kohut, who believed that the primary function of every human is to relate to other humans and the sole lifelong need is to develop and maintain a self, which is a matrix of ambition and empathy. When the caretakers of a child are neglectful, abusive, or emotionally indifferent, the child does not bond well and experiences traumatic empathic failures resulting in an arrested or undeveloped self. One's ambition is comprised of one's desire and level of initiative to achieve goals. One's talents and skills consist of the resources one has, while one's ideals consists of the final goals one wants to achieve. The family plays the primary role in a child's self. The extent that caretakers provide empathy, idealization, and sameness to the child is a crucial factor in a child's development. As a client *assimilates* with the therapist—transference by mirroring, idealizing, or sameness identification—a reparenting occurs, which allows a client to overcome dysfunctional behaviors. Kohut is seen as providing a therapeutic framework for the majority of psychotherapists.

For more information on self-psychology, go to www.selfpsychology.org or read *Object Relations and Self-psychology* (2000) by M. St. Clair or *The Analysis of the Self* (1971) by H. Kohut.

Adlerian/Individual Psychology: This was developed by Alfred Adler as he grew more critical of Freud, whom he had once largely supported. Adler believed that all behavior in one's life will be evidence of moving toward a goal of achieving superiority and will be characterized by degrees of social interest. This type of psychology believes that it is not what happens to a person that is important but how one perceives and uses creativity and experience that defines the human condition. What we take to be true is our reality. He believed there are four priorities in life (superiority, control, comfort, and pleasing— each of which have costs and benefits), as well as five tasks (love, work, friendship, self, and spirituality). To maximize health one needs to perceive and develop a sense of significance while feeling they are part of the whole. Healthy adults will strive for superiority by cooperating with others instead of competing with them. Adler's ideas have been incorporated into almost every school of therapy.

For more information on Adlerian/individual psychology, go to www.adler.edu or read *Counseling and Psychotherapy* 2000 by D. C. Dinkmeyer and L. Sperry.

Existential Counseling: This therapy grew out of belief that dehumanizing forces were at work in various fields, including scientific, industrial, psychiatric, and political arenas, resulting in a compartmentalization—family separated from work, religion distant from the daily drudgery, rigid gender roles, and humans being merely tools of production in the years prior to the World War I. Existential therapy involves a continual emerging, a transcending of one's past. Mental health is conceptualized as *authenticity*—an ongoing striving that accepts and even embraces the givens of life, such as death, isolation, freedom, and meaninglessness, as they play out in the four interrelated spheres of life: the physical world (Umwelt), the interpersonal world (Mitwelt), the personal world (Eigenwelt), and the spiritual world (Uberwelt). Gaining awareness and taking responsibility for confronting the givens of existence are the main goals of existential counseling.

For more information on existential counseling, go to www.existential.mcmail.com or read *Everyday Mysteries: Existential Dimensions in Psychotherapy* (1997) by E. van Deurzen-Smith.

Person-Centered Counseling: Carl Rogers began person-centered counseling during World War II and continued to refine it during his lifetime. He received the APA's first Distinguished Scientist Award in 1956. He saw humans to be essentially positive with the tendency to grow, heal, and develop one's full potential. He also believed everyone, to varying degrees, becomes alienated, and it is by affection, affiliation, aggression, and sex that one can once again begin to grow, heal, and continue to develop potential. He believed that receiving positive regard from others was more important than one's own value process. Due to his belief that virtually 100% of positive outcomes in psychotherapy comes from the quality of the therapeutic relationship, he set forth six necessary conditions for constructive personality change and the twelve steps of the counseling process.

For more information on person-centered counseling, go to www.personcentered.com or read *On Becoming a Person* (1961) by Carl Rogers.

Gestalt Counseling: *Gestalt Therapy: Excitement and Growth in the Human Personality* (1951) by Perls, Hefferline, and Goodman introduced Gestalt to America, although Fritz and Laura Perls had been practicing it in South Africa some years earlier. Meaning is best derived and understood by considering the individual's interpretation of immediate experience. Too much thinking gets in the way of true awareness and maturity. "To me nothing exists but the now. Now=experience=awareness=reality."[67] When one restricts awareness, patterns develop that fail to meet needs or are destructive to the self or others. Understanding the world from the perspective of the client, respecting the belief that each person has a unique perception of the self, the other, and the environment, is the focus of Gestalt. This understanding of the client's reality is the key for change. Due to Gestalt's active

41

nature and creative use of experiments, it is necessary that a counselor have adequate knowledge of the various techniques before incorporating them into a system of counseling.

For more information on Gestalt counseling, go to www. gestalt.org or read *Gestalt Therapy: Practice and Theory*, 2nd edition, (1989) by M. P. Korb, J. Gorrell, and V. Van De Riet.

Reality Therapy and Choice Theory: William Glasser began developing reality therapy during his time at UCLA in the 1960s, evolving it into choice theory by the 1990s. According to choice theory, the five basic needs are survival, love and belonging, power, fun, and freedom. These needs can interact and overlap, and each person has the ability to translate these needs into specific wants—the people, objects, or circumstances that meet their needs. These wants can be revised throughout life. The survival need is the only one that is not completely psychological. To satisfy every other need, we must have relations with other people. Satisfying the need for love and belonging is a key to satisfying all other needs. Power needs can be satisfied by a sense of accomplishment and competence. Fun is the quest for enjoyment—a playfulness and deep intimacy. Freedom is part of the desire for autonomy—the ability to make a choice from several relatively unrestricted options; often this involves creativity.

To Glasser, people exhibiting maladjustment were not to be considered as mentally ill, but examples of ways people choose to behave when they feel thwarted in the attempt to satisfy any of the five basic needs. What others consider to be mental illness, he saw as ways in which huge numbers of people choose to deal with the pain of loneliness or disconnection in order to avoid even greater pain. Choosing intense symptoms such as depression and anxiety keeps angering under control and enables people to avoid what they are afraid of doing.

A person's every behavior—thinking, doing, feeling, and physiology—constitute his or her best effort to meet his or her basic needs. Behaviors may be responsible or irresponsible and effective or ineffective. Responsible behavior fulfills ones needs without preventing others from fulfilling theirs. Irresponsible behaviors fulfill one's needs in a way that prevents others from fulfilling theirs. One can influence but not control others. If one wants to have the highest probability of successful change, one needs to target areas that one can control. Healthy functioning is characterized by responsible behavior.

For more information on choice theory, go to www. wglasserinst.com or read *Choice Theory* (1998) by William Glasser.

Behavioral Counseling: According to behavioral counseling, behavior consists of voluntary and involuntary behaviors as a result of experiences in the environment; every person is a passive product of his or her environment. Strict behaviorists believe that cognitive events are not significant in producing behaviors and that current behaviors are the result of events that occur before and after the behavior. Positive reinforcement is when reinforcement occurs shortly after some response that increases the likelihood of the response happening again. Negative reinforcement is when a response is taken to avoid something adverse. Dysfunctional behaviors arise from a failure to learn needed behaviors. Behavior changes when environmental contingencies change. Therapeutic punishments can be utilized by counselors to inhibit certain behaviors. These therapeutic punishments can range from time-outs— the separation from a group or activity—to mild electroshock, similar in strength to an elastic band being snapped on the wrist, or a two-second shock at 15.5 milliamps or even 45 milliamps, as used at the Judge Rotenberg Center (JRC) in Canton, Massachusetts (stun guns used by police deliver one to four milliamps), where clients can be shocked repeatedly[68] when in restraints or when lying writhing on the floor, occasionally causing death. Many, including myself, believe those who use such extreme methods are rather sadistic micromanaging individuals who should be charged with crimes, including that of torture and child abuse. As both the states of New York and Massachusetts send clients to JRC, perhaps the governors of those states should also be charged. Most behaviorists currently use a mix of behavioral and cognitive methods.

For more information on behavioral counseling, go to www. aabt.org or read *Contemporary Behavior Therapy* (2003) by M. D. Springer and D. C. Guevremont.

Cognitive Counseling: Cognitive counseling was developed by Aaron Temkin Beck in the early 1960s. Individuals have differing temperaments beginning at birth, and these differing temperaments push people in different directions. Individuals are active participants in their environments, evaluating various stimuli, interpreting events and sensations, judging their own responses, and actively seeking and creating goals. Individuals become distressed when they experience a threat to their interests. The greater the threat is perceived to one's well-being, the more intense the distress. Distress is a signal that one is not handling the pressure one faces very well. Much of cognitive therapy is about learning to deal better with the stresses one can face.

Schemas are the core phenomena that comprise the five survival supporting systems—cognitive, emotional, physiological, motivational, and behavioral. Cognitive schemas are beliefs about perceived danger, violation, loss, and gain. Emotional schemas are the core emotions: anxiety, anger, sadness, and joy. Physiological schemas are the core ways the body's autonomic, motor, and sensory systems are energized along with the emotions. Motivational schemas are the impulses to escape or avoid, to lash out, to grieve, or to seek and encounter. Behavioral schemas are core actions: shaking, scowling, crying, and smiling. Modes are the interrelated schemas and can be either major or minor, with the mode more energized being the major mode. A conscious control system is separate from modes and can be used to de-energize the modes. Schemas tend to develop early in childhood, and individuals tend to perpetuate the modeling they experienced in childhood.

For more information on cognitive counseling, go to www.schematherapy.com or read *Emotional Alchemy: How the Mind Can Heal the Heart* (2001) by Tara Bennett-Goleman. Information on this subject can also be found in my earlier book, *Mental Illness: A Guide to Recovery.*

Rational-Emotive Behavioral Therapy (REBT): REBT was developed by Albert Ellis from 1956 to 1993, undergoing several name changes as it was refined. Knowledge is based upon our selective interpretation of the world. How a person perceives people and events influences how the person feels, behaves, and thinks. Every person's truth or reality is internally defined and experienced. An essential of REBT is being flexible in one's worldview as others have their subjective views, which will differ from one's own. No conclusion can be based on all information, so views will need to be modified as new information becomes available. Enjoying life is a primary goal in REBT, and rational individuals strive to maximize pleasure, but as personal responsibility is also emphasized, short-term pleasures must at times be sacrificed for long-term goals. According to Ellis, people are influenced by two biological tendencies: to think and behave irrationally and to think and behave rationally, dispelling irrational beliefs in order to life a more rational, self-actualized life. One's environment has an impact on personality development, and many dysfunctional beliefs involving absolutes derive from injunctions received when young. Heredity is considered to play a role in psychological dysfunction, but neither nature nor nurture holds ultimate sway over an individual's thought process. Among the beliefs of REBT is free will, which is a privilege and a responsibility, knowing that *I alone* am responsible for personal feelings, thought, and actions. Your own experience is the highest authority. Be present in the moment. No one is perfect.

For more information on REBT, go to www.rebt.org or read *Reason and Emotion in Psychotherapy* (1962) by A. Ellis.

Buddhist Psychology

In Buddhism it is believed two types of people are prone to develop mental health problems.[69]

- Those who take on too much responsibility and consequently spend an enormous amount of time thinking
- Those who take on too little responsibility and spend little time developing their mental abilities

It is also believed that individuals have one of five vibrational aspects. One vibrational aspect is not better than any other, but contentment occurs when individuals pursue activities that are in harmony with that aspect. Not being in harmony with one's vibrational aspect will manifest itself in depression and self-destructive behaviors. The further out-of-harmony an individual is, the greater the tendency for destructive behaviors.

Vajrayana (Tibetan or Tantric) Buddhism is a contemplative tradition with an understanding of energy at its core and categorizes humans as having five basic qualities. Each energy expresses itself in personality traits we commonly classify as dysfunctional or neurotic and those we consider constructive or wise. Both troublesome and pleasant emotions arise out of this energetic matrix.

In *The Five Wisdom Energies: A Buddhist Way of Understanding Personalities, Emotions, and Relationships*, Irini Rockwell gives descriptions of the five energies and their colors, inherent wisdom, and confusion.

The *Buddha* family radiates a white energy and is spacious and peaceful. Buddha energy is an all-pervasive, peaceful space;

this is its wisdom quality. It can also be solidly immobile, with the density of ignoring or denying; that is its confused quality.

The *vajra* family reflects a blue energy. Like a crystal clear mirror, *vajra* reflects what it sees without bias. But it also has a self-righteousness that can harden into cold or hot anger.

The *ratna* family exudes a rich and earthy golden-yellow energy that encompasses everything. The wisdom quality of *ratna* energy is richness, equanimity, and satisfaction. But it can also turn into greedy territoriality and puffed-up pride.

The *padma* family glows with the vitality of red energy. *Padma's* passion is, at its best, compassionate wisdom. It is finely tuned in to what is happening, without bias. However, when neurotic, it can cling obsessively to what gives pleasure. While politicians, salesmen, and even some psychologists consider being sexy, smooth talking, and insincere desirable characteristics, these combined traits are considered to be on the neurotic side of *padma*, not on the wise or constructive side.

The *karma* family emits a green energy and is swift and energetic like the wind. *Karma* energy is all-accomplishing action for the benefit of others. But it can become power-hungry, manipulative, competitive, and envious.

Postures and colors can aid in the breaking of habitual patterns, which can be locked in the body for years. These postures and colors are designed to intensify and transmute specific neurotic patterns.

More information, including videos and slideshows can be found at www.fivewisdomsinstitute.com.

Somatic Experiencing (SE)

SE is a body-awareness approach to trauma being taught throughout the world. It is the result of over forty years of observation, research, and hands-on development by Dr. Peter Levine. Based upon the realization that human beings have an innate ability to overcome the effects of trauma, SE employs awareness of body sensation to help people "renegotiate" and heal rather than relive or reenact trauma.

- SE's guidance of the bodily "felt sense" allows the highly aroused survival energies to be safely experienced and gradually discharged.
- SE "titrates" experience rather than evoking catharsis—which can overwhelm the regulatory mechanisms of the organism. (Basically this means it takes place at a rate the patient can satisfactorily tolerate without reliving the trauma.)
- SE helps eliminate pitfalls of retraumatization and the spurious generation of "false memories."

A compulsion can develop to repeat the actions that caused the problem in the first place. We are inextricably drawn into situations that replicate the original trauma in both obvious and less obvious ways. The prostitute or stripper with a history of childhood sexual abuse is a common example. We may find ourselves re-experiencing the effects of trauma either through physical symptoms or through a full-blown interaction with the external environment . . . . Once he became aware of his feelings and the role the original event had played in driving his compulsion, the man was able to stop re-enacting this tragic incident.[70]

More information on somatic experiencing can be found at www.traumahealing.com or through contacting the Somatic Experiencing Trauma Institute, 6685 Gunpark Drive Suite 102, Boulder, CO 80301 (phone: 303-652-4035).

Eye Movement Desensitization and Reprocessing (EMDR)

EMDR is considered to be evidence-based according to the Substance Abuse and Mental Health Services Administration (SAMHSA). Counseling is only a small portion of this therapy, which was developed for children. It is briefer than most programs designed to treat trauma, rarely lasting more than four or five sessions. It also works with adults. This method of treating trauma doesn't require the patient to divulge all information regarding the trauma to the provider. While the client recalls the incidents in his or her mind, the eyes are guided in a smooth pattern. Individuals I know who have undergone this therapy claim that it has been successful about 50% of the time. Some therapists claim an 80% success rate, while literature on the subject claim that clinicians who rush the process have lower success rates. The International EMDR Association (http://www. emdria.org) establishes standards for EMDR, while the EMDR Institute (www.emdr.com) provides a directory of trained EMDR clinicians and compiles information on workshops, seminars, and research.

Tension and Trauma Releasing Exercises (TRE)

TRE is a simple technique that uses exercises to release stress or tension from the body that accumulate from everyday circumstances of life, from difficult situations, immediate or prolonged stressful situations, or traumatic life experiences (e.g., natural disasters, social or domestic violence).

TRE is a set of six exercises that help to release deep tension from the body by evoking a self-controlled muscular shaking process in the body called neurogenic muscle tremors. The uniqueness of this technique is that this shaking originates deep in the core of the body of the psoas muscles. These gentle tremors reverberate outward along the spine, releasing tension from the sacrum to the cranium. The exercises are a simple form of stretching and are used to gently trigger these voluntary muscle tremors. Eventually, these tremors will evoke themselves naturally in a rest position to reduce any stress or tension that was accumulated over the course of the day.

> *A traumatized individual tends to lack the ability to rate their fears on a graded scale and thereby put them in perspective. When a person lacks the normal gradations of fear, any occurrence of fear is immediately translated into terror. The individual's reaction will be overly defensive, likely in the form of an outburst of anger, tears, or withdrawal into isolation and even depression.*[71]

For more information on TRE, see www.traumaprevention. com or www.TREcalifornia.com or read the book *The Revolutionary Trauma Release Process: Transcend Your Toughest Times* by David Berceli, PhD.

WRAP

Mentioned in chapter 1, the Wellness Recovery Action Plan (WRAP) is a self-management and recovery system developed by a group of people who had mental health difficulties and who were struggling to incorporate wellness tools and strategies into their lives. WRAP is designed to

- decrease and prevent intrusive or troubling feelings and behaviors,
- increase personal empowerment,
- improve quality of life,
- assist people in achieving their own life goals and dreams.

WRAP is a structured system to monitor uncomfortable and distressing feelings and behaviors and, through planned responses, to reduce, modify, or eliminate them. It also includes plans for responses from others when you cannot make decisions, take care of yourself, or keep yourself safe. WRAP is especially helpful when a trauma occurred at a young age. One of the difficulties young individuals have in dealing with trauma is that one emotion, even one that is considered positive, can set off a negative emotion. For example, if a group of children are having a party, laughing and having a good time, when a car comes crashing through a fence, killing or injuring one or more children, aside from the immediate reactions to the accident, at a later date some individuals may go into a state of fear when he or she laughs or hears laughter as it can trigger memories of the crash. Later, the person may go right to fear when exposed to laughter without recalling the accident, particularly if the accident occurred when the individual was quite young. WRAP works primarily by helping individuals sort out conflicting emotions.

For more information on WRAP, go to http://copelandcenter. com/wellness-recovery-action-plan-wrap. Various training information is available.

LEAP

This program can be found in *I Am Not Sick, I Don't Need Help* by Dr. Xavier Amador. Dr. Amador essentially took some common principles from the disability community on learning how to deal with life when a disability becomes part of one's life and fine-tuned them to meet the needs of those who have received a mental health diagnosis. While this program is especially helpful for those individuals who have developed resistance to the idea that their thoughts, behaviors, and actions may be impeding their enjoyment of life, and don't believe they have a mental illness, it is also quite useful in bringing people to agreement on the best way to proceed when disagreements present themselves.

The basics of this program are listening, empathizing, agreeing, and partnership. Communication skills can work to aid an individual in recovery develop a treatment plan and get him or her back on it should they relapse. It shows how to gain the trust of someone you are at odds with by stop trying to convince the other person he is wrong or simply misguided and instead listen in a new way that conveys respect for the person's point of view. It results in a lowering of tension, anger, and defensiveness. As genuine understanding, empathy, and respect for his point of view are conveyed, you are able to find common ground on which you can partner. As this occurs, the opinions and advice that were previously rejected begin to be considered.

More information on LEAP can be found at http://www.leapinstitute.org/leap-videos/ or by reading Dr. Amador's book *I Am Not Sick, I Don't Need Help.*

The NAMI Peer Recovery Program

The NAMI Peer to Peer Recovery Program was created by Kathryn McNulty. It is a ten-week scripted course designed to help individuals prevent relapse by recognizing symptoms and events that may trigger a downward spiral. It is most beneficial when an individual has recognized that something is not going right in his or her life and wishes to improve his or her circumstances. It is a peer course requiring least two, preferably three, peers who have completed a course by NAMI trainers.

Each class contains a combination of lecture and interactive exercise material and closes with a mindfulness practice (techniques offered to develop and expand awareness). Each class builds on the one before: attendance each week is strongly recommended.

Major topics covered are mental illnesses as traumatic experiences, stages of recovery, brain biology and research, challenges and benefits of medication, relapse prevention, mindfulness, substance abuse and addiction, role of acceptance in recovery, understanding emotions, focusing on experiences of joy, spirituality, physical health and mental health, suicide and prevention, and advance directives. Discussions about the various mental health diagnoses can be quite lively and informative.

A video about this peer-to-peer program can be found at http://www.youtube.com/watch?feature=player_embedded&v =XoHsAe2lBRs.

More information about this peer-to-peer program and other NAMI programs can be found at http://www.nami.org/template. cfm?section=Peer-to-Peer.

Emotional CPR

Emotional CPR (E-CPR) is an educational program designed to teach people to assist others through an emotional crisis by three simple steps: C = connecting, P = empowering, and R = revitalizing. The connecting process of E-CPR involves deepening listening skills, practicing presence, and creating a sense of safety for the person experiencing a crisis. The empowering process helps people better understand how to feel empowered themselves and assists others to feel more hopeful and engaged in life. In the revitalizing process, people reengage in relationships with their loved ones or their support system, and they resume or begin routines that support health and wellness. This reinforces the person's sense of mastery and accomplishment, further energizing the healing process. E-CPR was developed by the National Coalition for Mental Health Recovery, endorsed by the Commission on Accreditation of Rehabilitation Facilities (CARF), and recommended by the International Association of Chiefs of Police (IACP):

> *Law enforcement personnel who learn E-CPR will be better equipped to efficiently and effectively resolve a crisis call involving people in emotional distress, thereby*

reducing potential escalation, harm, or injury. E-CPR is recommended by the IACP as a way to enrich Crisis Intervention Training (CIT) curricula.[72]

A video and other information on Emotional CPR can be found at http://www.emotional-cpr.org/videos.htm.

How to Deal with Difficult People

While not a counseling program, the video series, *How To Deal With Difficult People*,[73] can help individuals recognize and correct difficult behaviors and aid in determining an individual's propensity for certain antisocial behaviors. The grid used is a simplified system that correlates where a person is on the grid to various types of difficult behavior and does so in a humorous, nonthreatening way.

Everyone falls someplace along the continuum, from passive to aggressive. Likewise, everyone falls someplace along the line of being task-oriented or people-oriented. Those who have developed the skills to be near the center, as well as having the ability to change according to circumstances, tend to be well adjusted and generally have few problems dealing with people. The further away from the center a person is, a tendency develops to encounter increasingly more difficult people; this is because they are becoming other people's difficult person. Yet everyone has a positive intent. Understanding this intent is the first step in getting them to collaborate.

The **Tank** is pushy, rude, loud, and forceful, although they can also attack with surgical precision. If you are in their way, you will be run over (ruler quadrant).

The **Know-It-All**, usually quite knowledgeable at least in some area, can take hours of your time in imposing their views while considering your viewpoint as inferior (ruler quadrant).

The **Sniper** gets even by identifying your weaknesses and exploiting them by sabotage, gossip, and put-downs (ruler quadrant). The friendly Sniper uses *sniping* as a fun way to get attention (entertainer quadrant).

The **Grenade** explodes in tantrums that seem out of proportion to the matter at hand. Residing in the entertainer quadrant, *Grenades* can blow up at unexpected moments whenever they believe their need for appreciation may be thwarted (entertainer quadrant).

The **Think-They-Know-It-All**, usually with just one small piece of information, will hammer away with it, typically sending the project at hand into the trash bin (entertainer quadrant).

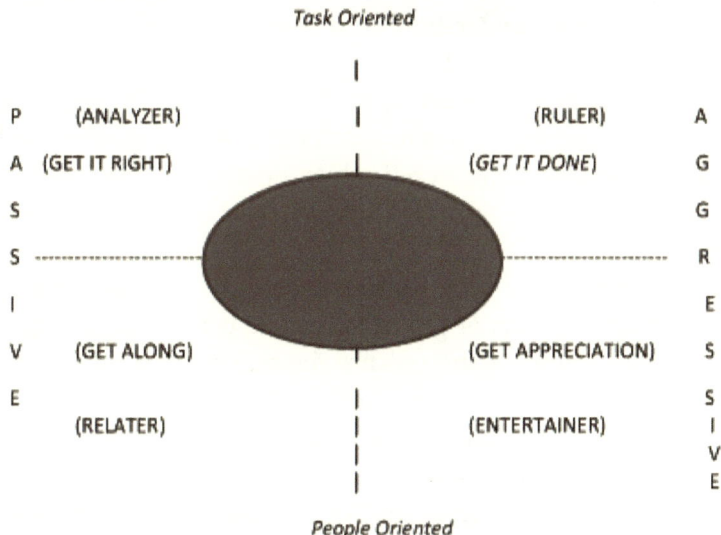

Task Oriented

P	(ANALYZER)	(RULER)	A
A	(GET IT RIGHT)	(GET IT DONE)	G
S			G
S			R
I			E
V	(GET ALONG)	(GET APPRECIATION)	S
E			S
	(RELATER)	(ENTERTAINER)	I
			V
			E

People Oriented

The **Yes person** is quick to agree but may never follow through. While they agree in order to please others, they usually leave others disappointed (relater quadrant).

The **Maybe person** puts crucial decisions off until it is too late to do anything. Either events or someone else will make decisions (relater quadrant).

The **Nothing person** withdraws, never gives feedback, wants to avoid conflict, and may have valuable information that may be of aid (analyzer and relater quadrants).

The **No person** brings defeat to every project. Nothing can possibly be accomplished, so why try? (analyzer quadrant).

The **Whiner** is certain everything is wrong and will never be set right. Believing himself to be realistic, he is willing and ready to drag everyone down (analyzer quadrant).

Yet each of these difficult people can be turned into a helpful asset. The video helps you learn how.

I found the *How To Deal With Difficult People* video series to be an excellent aid when used during counseling sessions. Some of the so-called mentally ill are simply individuals who primarily have learned poor reactions to stress. This video series can have individuals better understand how minor changes can vastly improve their quality of life.

A short booklet containing the basics of *How To Deal with Difficult People* can be downloaded at http://www.freewebs.com/wasimexpress4/dealdifficult.pdf, while short videos and ordering information can be found at http://rickbrinkman.com/store/videos/.

The *How To Deal With Difficult People* grid can also be used to understand actions of groups of people better. For instance, those in law enforcement and fire fighting often need to take direct deliberate actions without getting permissions from various sources first. Standing by and doing nothing when lives are in danger is not an option for them. They need to be able to move into the *ruler* category. Yet if called on too often to act quickly, they can grow accustomed to operating quickly and forcefully even when it is not called for. They need to be able to center themselves and even say no to political leaders at times to continue having the trust of the people. Unnecessarily rash actions can have long-term negative consequences.

When I was about twenty, my father told me about his day. He responded to a call about a man with a gun. A sixteen-year-old had a single shot .22 and was threatening to kill his parents. He was outside the home on a second-story landing. He approached the kid and talked to him for about twenty minutes before the kid handed my father his rifle. Immediately, several cops who had gathered at the bottom of the stairs rushed up, grabbed the kid, dragged him down the stairs, cuffed him, and threw him in the patrol car. My father was near tears as he said, "That kid will never trust a cop again as long as he lives." The undue force used likely turned that kid into someone who would distrust and fear the police, viewing them as the enemy. Unfortunately, today we have many hundreds of thousands—millions—who no longer trust the police, and many have good reason.

Those who favor quick and sometimes rash actions, erring on the side of too much force, even when the danger is over, currently seem to be attracted to the right wing of the political spectrum. The left wing seems to favor Yes people and Maybe people who never speak up to bosses, no matter what may seem to be going wrong, and tend to build fiefdoms in bureaucracies, doling out favors to clients who kiss up to them while denying various services to those who question them. Perhaps the current veterans administration scandal could have been avoided if Yes people and Maybe people were screened out of government jobs. Many psychiatrists seem to fall into the Know-It-All category.

Nonviolent Communication[74]

Nonviolent communication (NVC) is founded on developing language and communication skills that strengthen our ability to remain human, even under trying conditions. It contains nothing new but rather helps us reframe how we express ourselves and hear others. Instead of being habitual automatic reactions, our words become conscious responses based firmly on an awareness of what we are perceiving, feeling, and wanting. We are led to express ourselves with honesty and clarity while simultaneously paying others respectful and empathic attention. NVC is based on the principles of nonviolence—the natural state of compassion when no violence is present in the heart.

An excerpt from the course is as follows:

> *Respect for Authority involves three ingredients. We get respect for our authority when:*
> 1. *We know some things or can do some things the people we are working with or living with do not have.*
> 2. *The people see these things as valuable. They see how these things will enrich their lives.*
> 3. *They see us as offering these things; not imposing them.*
>
>   *Fear of authority is something different. It is when it is built into the structure . . . which gives us the right to impose things on people—reward or punish people to have people to do what we want.*
>
>   *Respect for authority needs to be earned . . . People can see the value in what we are offering. Another difference is to know the difference between obedience and willing cooperation. Obedience is maintained when people submit because we have the power to reward or punish. Willing cooperation can only be received when people feel free from this kind of coercion and they trust that their needs as human beings are valued. When they feel that they are open to whatever authority we have that might be valuable.*

For more information on the Nonviolent Communication Training Course, go to www.cnvc.org.

A video about Nonviolent Communication can be found at http://www.youtube.com/watch?v=-dpk5Z7GIFs.

Healing Grief

Those experiencing mental health problems can be experiencing grief. While a certain amount of grief can be expected in life, currently many of those identified as having mental health problems have been grieving the loss of a meaningful future (jail, prison, homelessness, forced drugging, institutionalization, poverty, and often anger at "the system") as a result of our current mental health treatment protocols and often erroneous diagnoses. Despite improvements in the past twenty years, mental health treatment can consist of little more than scolding individuals for not being compliant with a drug regimen regardless of whether they were adhering to it or not. This has been a factor both in people leaving treatment and enduring relapses. Family members can also experience grief at the time of diagnosis and renewed grief when their family member experiences a relapse or fails to develop age-related skills. The journey from shock to acceptance is perhaps the greatest obstacle on the road to recovery.

There are six stages of grief:[75] shock, denial, bargaining, anger, guilt, and acceptance.

I recommend *Healing Grief* by James Van Praagh (2001) for anyone interested in helping anyone, including oneself, heal from the grief they may be experiencing. Videos on healing grief can be found at various websites, including the following:

- http://www.youtube.com/watch?v=98rOW5inlnE
- Understanding Grief from the Hospice Foundation of America: http://www.griefhealingblog.com/2011/02/understanding-grief-new-video-from.html
- 155 Healing Attitudes about Healing Grief: http://www.youtube.com/watch?v=UWXlABRm6Lc

Books, videos, and other materials can also be found at http://www.vanpraagh.com/store/book/healing-grief-reclaiming-life-after-any-loss.

Transforming Anger[76]

Where there is anger, apply loving kindness. Avoid rash action. Be restrained in speech. Avoid mental agitation. Think good thoughts.

I encountered this method of transforming anger some years ago and consider myself fortunate to have done so. It has one requirement, to be honest with yourself, and four steps. It took me four months to work through the first three steps the first time. After that it became easier, but it still took me several years of working this method before I did not daily experience anger over the indignities I had endured. With practice, this method can be utilized mentally when a situation arises and triggers anger. This book can be considered part of my fourth step in this program.

Step one: The first step is to write down what is making you angry. Take your time with this. If you have a lot of things making you angry, pick the one making you the angriest. If you find yourself getting angry as you write, take a break. Go out for a walk or do something you feel calming. Tell yourself, "I'm addressing my anger, I'm working to resolve my anger." Take the time you need. Then go back and continue writing. Write down all the details about it. When you think you're done, ask yourself, "Anything else?" Write it down. At times I found that I could work only for a minute or less before I needed to take a break.

Step two: Ask yourself, "Did I contribute anything to this situation?" Write down all the contributions you made. It may be 80% of the situation, or it may only be 1% or 2%. Write it down. When you think you are done, ask yourself, "Anything else?" If you think of anything else, write it down. If you find yourself getting angry as you write, take a break.

Step three: Ask yourself, "What was the other person's perspective?" Write it down. "What was the other person's view of what happened?" Did that other person see some danger to themselves or one of their loved ones? What was the other person's perspective? Was the other person doing the best he or she could? Write it down. "Was the other person in over their head? Was the other person dealing with a new situation?"

Sometimes it isn't a person you may be angry with. If you're angry with God, ask yourself, "What was God's perspective?" Were you being given a challenge to overcome? Are you being requested to improve your life or the lives of others? If the answer feels right to you, it is the right answer. Again, if you find yourself getting angry, take a break and remind yourself that you are working to transform your anger.

Step four: Anger is a perceived injustice. If you have gotten this far and still feel anger, either you hid something from yourself along the way or an injustice was done. Anger is also energy stored in the body. It will seek action. It is up to individuals to find ways to release this energy in such ways that will benefit themselves and society. Many organizations have been founded to help people who are angry about an injustice they have suffered. Most wish to include others who have the same or similar objectives. Look for one that was formed to address the issues you have identified. Many have helped to make substantial changes. But if you can't find one that addresses your need, consider starting such a group yourself. Write down what you can do to make things better for someone else who may be in a similar situation, and then do it. Much work needs to be done to prevent anger from overcoming reason.

If you recognize that you were a contributor to the situation that made you angry, your anger should be reduced, but to bring greater joy into your life, work toward helping others.

Where there is anger, apply loving kindness. Avoid rash action. Be restrained in speech. Avoid mental agitation. Think good thoughts. Trauma can result in shrinkage of the hippocampus, which is adjacent to the amygdala, and can be considered the emotional center of the brain. This shrinkage affects the communication between areas of the brain and is responsible for heightened fear and anger responses. For this reason, it is recommended that individuals who have experienced significant trauma take courses on managing anger.

A short video of this method can be found at http://youtu.be/S8WB4KIn5qs.

64 Theoretical Models of Counseling and Psychotherapy. p. 17, 2004 by Kevin A. Fall, PhD, Janice Miner Holden, EdD, Andre Marquis, PhD.

65 2001, revised 2004, Gary Baran and CNVC. The right to freely duplicate this document is hereby granted.

66 The Road Less Traveled by M.Scott Peck, MD, 1978, 2002; pp. 16–17

67 Four Lectures *Gestalt therapy now* F. Perls, New York, Harper, p. 14

68 Disabled children at Mass. school are tortured, not treated (MA, Judge Rotenberg Center) FRIDAY, 01 OCTOBER 2010 http://www.cafety.org/publically-funded-programs/811-disabled-children-at-mass-school-are-tortured-not-treated--ma-judge-rotenberg-center-, 31 Shocks Later, New York Magazine Sep 2, 2012 http://nymag.com/news/features/andre-mccollins-rotenberg-center-2012-9/

69 Journey Without Goal, The Tantric Wisdom of the Buddha, by Chogyam Trungpa and The Five Wisdom Energies By Irini Rockwell 2002

70 *Healing Trauma by Peter Levine PhD, 2005 (pp. 20, 22)*

71 The Revolutionary Trauma Release Process, p. 91, 2008 by David Berceli PhD.

72 For more information on E-CPR go to: http://www.emotional-cpr.org/videos.htm#Emotional-CPR-Webinar.

73 How To Deal With Difficult People by Dr. Rick Brinkman and Dr. Rick Kirschner, 1982, Available at www.CareerTrack.com and http://rickbrinkman.com/store/

74 The Nonviolent Communication Training Course 2006 by Marshall Rosenberg, For more info on the Nonviolent Communication Training Course go to: www.cnvc.org.

75 Healing Grief by James Van Praagh 2001

76 adapted from The Art of Happiness by His Holiness the Dalai Lama and Howard C. Cutler 1998

CHAPTER 3

THE MEDICINE OF THE FUTURE IS NOW AVAILABLE

Major Differences between Conventional Medicine's and Vibrational Medicine's Worldviews

(From *Vibrational Medicine for the 21st Century* by Richard Gerber, MD)

Conventional Medicine	Vibrational Medicine
Based on Newtonian physics	Based on Einsteinian and quantum physics
Views the body as a biomachine	Views the body as a dynamic energy system
Sees the brain as a biocomputer with consciousness as a by-product of the brain's electrical energy	Mind and spirit as true sources of consciousness (the actual operators who run the brain/biocomputer)
Emotions thought to influence illness through neurohormonal connections between brain and body	Emotions and Spirit can influence illness via energetic and neurohormonal connections among mind, body, and spirit
Treatments with drugs and surgery to "fix" abnormal biomechanisms	Treatments with different forms and frequencies of energy to rebalance the physical body-mind-spirit complex

Vibrational medicine is a term that has not caught on outside of relatively small circles but is essentially part of integrative medicine (next topic), with a focus on how vibrations can work to heal on the cellular level. Various energy medicines, such as Reiki, and others can be considered forms of vibrational medicine, as is prayer. Perhaps the most interesting theory advanced in Vibrational Medicine for the 21st Century from the mental health perspective is that the body's electromagnetic field contains a communication system for both internal and external communication. Imbalances in this field are a possible reason for the phenomenon of "hearing voices" and possibly other symptoms as well.

The scientific rationale for vibrational medicine has two components. The first is that all matter, from the subatomic level to the universe and everything in between, vibrates. Light can be viewed as either a particle or a wave. According to Einstein's $E=mc^2$ formula, energy and matter are the same. The second is that the universe is holographic in nature. If you take a holographic picture of an object and cut it into a hundred pieces, the smallest piece will still contain the entire picture, although it will be fainter. While this rationale has not been fully embraced by the traditional medical community, it is being studied and accepted by an ever-growing number of scientists and physicians. Breakthroughs in this field should create a revolution in health care treatment. A portion of vibrational medicine is well-known: the placebo effect. While vibrational medicine is much more than that, the placebo effect is seen as resulting from the harmonizing effect of believing a cure is being put in place and from the confidence one has in the physician.

Vibrational medicine has similarities to the shamanic worldview. In shamanic cultures every person is believed to have four bodies (physical, mental, emotional, and spiritual) or aspects. Only one—the physical—is typically visible. When these four bodies are in harmony, a person has health. The more these bodies become imbalanced, disease results. Shamans had the responsibility of helping to maintain or restore harmony so the community would prosper. Vibrational medicine works to enhance harmony in the mind-body complex.

Ancient systems of medicine often have large elements of vibrational medicine contained within them. While some attack these systems for using parts of endangered species within some of their remedies, perhaps investigations into which remedies can be attributed solely to the placebo effect and which have greater success rates could help the transition away from utilizing endangered species.

Integrative Medicine

Integrative medicine[77] combines conventional care with alternative medicine to improve patient care. Rather than practice one type of medicine, integrative physicians will often combine therapies and treatment approaches to ensure the best results for their patients. Integrative physicians do not shun Western medicine; they practice Western care every day. These physicians are unique in that they incorporate appropriate and proven alternative treatment options. The types of medicine employed by integrative medicine physicians are as follows: Western medicine, allopathic medicine, osteopathic medicine, regenerative medicine, holistic medicine, naturopathic medicine, and functional medicine. Integrating the numerous therapies, often called alternative or complementary, into the medical system is a goal of integrative medicine. At the current time some practitioners of conventional medicine view integrative medicine with distrust as these methods are not typically covered in the coursework needed for a conventional medical degree. They can be more time-consuming than typical office visits and are not as dependent on the drugs, which physicians typically prescribe.

Greater use of integrative medicine can work to allay the fears of those with mental health diagnoses. Aside from often having concerns about being homeless or nearly so, having little prospect for employment, and daily facing discrimination and stigma, they also have to deal with the fact that powerful people and organizations advocate rounding them up and forcing drugs upon them. These forced treatment proponents do little more than provide scapegoats for a public scared with misleading information while providing no solution other than instituting fascism in America. Providing options for a viable future will lower the stress level of an already overstressed segment of the population and begin to restore dignity and compassion to the American vocabulary.

Ayurveda

Ayurveda is the main system of healing in India. It is as much a way of life as a system of medicine and encompasses science, religion, and philosophy. It generally falls within the scope of vibrational medicine as do most ancient healing systems. Its ultimate aim is to promote self-realization and a harmonious relationship with the world. In Ayurveda all aspects of existence are considered pure intellect or consciousness. Energy and matter are one. Energy is manifested in five elements: ether, air, fire, water, and earth. The five elements combine to form three basic forces known as *tridoshas* and somewhat resemble the four humors (personality types), which were the foundation of Western medicine until the Cartesian mind-body split in the seventeenth century. When a *dosha* imbalance is diagnosed, the first step is to eliminate toxins in the body. Subsequent treatments fall into three main categories: medicines from natural sources, dietary regimens, and behavioral modifications. Ayurveda has attracted increasing attention from medical scientists in the West and in Japan. The World Health Organization promotes its practice in developing countries.

Chinese Medicine

While Chinese medicine includes acupuncture, acupressure, and herbal remedies among others, it possibly can be summed up with an ancient formula: practice + intention = inner harmony + qi (chi) flow = health and longevity. In the Western medicine is for the treatment of disease. Chinese medicine also has that, but it has another category sometimes referred to as "enhance the righteous," which is meant to maximize what is right rather than to fix what is wrong. In Chinese medicine, qi is believed to be the life force itself. It is free and available to anyone, everywhere contained within the air and within all things. It can be in three possible states: harmony, deficiency, and stagnation, which determine the degree of health or disease. The goal of Chinese medicine is to increase harmony.

Craniosacral Therapy

Craniosacral therapy is perhaps the most promising of the integrative modalities for the treatment of any illness that stems from brain dysfunction. Developed by John Upledger, DO, OMM, director of the Upledger Institute, Palm Beach Gardens, Florida, it is a combination of a light-touch massage along with vibrational medicine, which acts to increase the flow of the cerebrospinal fluid, which bathes the brain in nutrients and washes away waste material. During a preliminary study using this therapy with children with autism, his young patients showed remarkable short-term behavior improvements, but the study was never completed. Additionally his findings seem to suggest that the intracranial membrane system of children with autism was preventing the meninges from accommodating the normal growth process, inhibiting the flow of cerebrospinal fluid.[78] This therapy has significant implications for the treatment of the various brain dysfunctions but requires more research.

Sound Therapy Using Tuning Forks

Sound therapy using tuning forks[79] was developed by Ardin Wilken and uses a series of specially designed tuning forks. During sessions the tuning forks, which are in harmony with each other (perfect fifths) are placed, one by each ear, producing a calm, relaxing effect in 97–98% of individuals by sending a third-resonance frequency through the bones and connective tissues. Aside from aiding individuals fall asleep, it creates a standing wave in the cerebrospinal fluid, which helps to regenerate this fluid and flush our waste products produced by the brain.[80] Problems sleeping are common among individuals with a mental health diagnosis. While not as effective as individual therapy, CDs are available. This is another therapy that could benefit many at low cost but needs to be properly researched. There is an institute in Barcelona, Spain, and another outside of London, England that are doing research.

Homeopathic Medicine

Homeopathic medicine can generally be considered within the field of vibrational medicine as are both Chinese medicine and Ayurveda. Homeopathic remedies are diluted until the physical properties of the original herb are removed (not even a single atom of the original substance is present), which leaves only the subtle energies or vibrational aspect of the original substance. The matching of the frequency of the illness with the frequency of the plant extract is now thought to be the principle behind the workings of homeopathic remedies. Homeopathic physicians view themselves as facilitators of healing rather than as healers. Until the end of World War I, homeopathic doctors and hospitals were more common than allopathic (currently considered traditional) doctors. While they had substantial success in treating patients, they were unable to provide a scientific rationale for why their methods worked. Thus, they were decried as not being scientifically based. Now that the rationale has been provided and that a heavy cultural bias has been dropped, there has been a resurgence of interest in this field.

Meditation

Meditation has been proven to increase activity in the left prefrontal cortex of the brain. Individuals with greater activity in the left prefrontal cortex have been found to be happier and more content than those with a more active right prefrontal cortex. The latter are more likely to display spontaneous antisocial behavior (anger, violence, and withdrawal).[81] While other benefits accrue from meditation, this alone should be reason enough to encourage it. Some individuals do experience greater anxiety during meditation. For them walking meditation is generally recommended, where the mind's focus is on the movement of the feet, not on the breath as it generally is for sitting meditation. Meditation can also be considered within the field of vibrational medicine.

> *Dr. Lazar's team hypothesized that long-term meditation practice might also result in changes in the brain's physical structure, possibly reflecting increased use of specific brain regions. In fact, they found that brain regions associated with attention, interoception (sensitivity to stimuli originating inside the body), and sensory processing were thicker in the meditation participants than they were in matched controls. These areas included the prefrontal cortex, which is responsible for planning complex cognitive behaviors, and the right anterior insula, which is associated with bodily sensations and emotions. "As predicted," says Dr. Lazar, "the brain regions associated with attention and sensory processing were thicker in meditators than in the controls. These findings provide*

the first evidence that alterations in brain structure are associated with meditation practice."[82]

Vitamin C

"A considerable list of bacterial, parasitic, and other non-viral infections continues to plague mankind. Many respond poorly to antibiotics or do not respond at all. . . . [High dosages of intravenous] vitamin C has been shown to prevent, speed recovery, and even cure many of these infections." Partial listing of such infections includes diphtheria, dysentery, leprosy, malaria, pertussis, pneumonia, pseudomonas infections, rheumatic fever, staph infections, strep infections, tetanus, trichinosis, tuberculosis, and typhoid fever.[83] Vitamin C, too, is considered to be a significant factor in recovery from cancer.

Perception-Shifting Exercises[84]

Luis Diaz, in his book *Memory in the Cells: How to Heal Our Behavioral Patterns and Release the Pain Body* presents some wonderfully simple perspective-shifting exercises. Being able to make these perception shifts may increase health and may help it easier for one to find joy in one's life.

The following information on cellular memory is reprinted with permission.

> *The Cellular Memory is the blueprint for your existence. It is the energetic expression of you as a holistic being. The labels "mind," "body" and "spirit" are artificial labels that exist to make it easier for you to comprehend your multidimensional existence on earth. Each point within your cellular memory contains all the information of the whole. This information is infinitely accessible to each*

and every cell of your body. If you magnify your cells down to your atoms, you would see that you are made up of subtle bundles of "info-energy." This info-energy is comprised of physical, mental and emotional data that comes from all of your life experiences, genetic heritage, and past generations. Nothing we experience escapes being imprinted into our Cellular Hologram in the form of a cell memory. What we commonly refer to as "The Cellular Memory" is the collective energy field generated by these individual cell memories. It operates behind the scenes of our subconscious mind.

The Cellular Memory pre-disposes or "programs" you to perceive and behave a certain way as thoughts and feelings are made manifest within your consciousness. To use the analogy of a computer, the holistic being-ness is the hard disk, or storage disk. The Cellular Memory is the database on the storage disk. The files within the database are the **cell memories**. It can be stated that everything that has ever happened to us is recorded in the cells of our body similarly to files being stored within a computer. In this way, the Cellular Memory is a biocomputer that influences our relationships to everything and anything that is happening. It affects the way we perform routine tasks and how we react to stress and handle emotional challenges in our present circumstances. Stored within the Cellular Memory are all the conscious and unconscious patterns of behaviors. The unproductive patterns impair our ability to feel well, happy, healthy, attain our goals and fulfill our destiny.

By default, your body is built to support health, harmony and connection between all parts. So why do we get sick, develop a disease or illness that won't easily go away? If our bodies are meant to support vitality and healing then why doesn't it just happen right away? The simplest answer in our experience over the last 20 years is that the Cellular Memory by nature contains both Positive

Emotional Charge (PEC) and Negative Emotional Charge (NEC) that is constantly flowing and influencing our state of mind and body health. The PEC is our soul's birthright. It can be described as an energy field of life force that is free flowing, expanding, peaceful, non-fearful, whole and alive beyond words.

The NEC is our human condition. It can be described as an energy field of life force that is contracted; held as unprocessed traumatic experiences, negative beliefs about ourselves and others, suffocation, fear and any emotion that is a derivation of fear such as guilt, grief, shame, embarrassment, resentment, anger, etc. We refer to the NEC's collective energy field as the Pain Body. When the NEC becomes disproportionably higher than the PEC, this leads to massive dysfunction in the human body-mind system.

Energy contractions in the cellular memory is the make-up of the pain body. Unconscious patterns that are hurting us feed the pain body and keep it unknown to us. The pain body is sometimes obvious (rage), tricky (sarcasm), or hidden (depression). When it comes out it always creates more pain in the cells. When we transform these unconscious repetitive patterns our cells begin to release the contractions, and we return to experiencing and living from the place of our original design—the light body. This transformation may require us to open up and release suppressed energies in us.

Pain Body Release (PBR).

- When something insignificant stimulates an enormous response.
- When there are uncomfortable feelings sensations like a turbulence, a constriction, a hole or emptiness, heaviness, heat, dizziness, a stabbing feeling, a ball in the throat, burning, etc.

- *It is addictive. When it takes over us the last thing we want is peace. We want to complain, criticize or defend.*
- *The pain body attracts the drama in our lives. The majority of our relationships are built on a drama foundation.*

Candace Pert, former chief of the section of brain biochemistry of the Clinical Neuroscience Branch at the National Institute of Mental Health, studies health influences at the neurochemical level. She noted recently that "repressing emotions can only be causative of disease. Failure to find effective ways to express negative emotions causes you to 'stew in your own juices.'"

Day after day, this chronic immersion in negativity is what appears to produce harmful influences on health.

> Could this be the reason for burnout in jobs with frequent negative people contact?

The key, according to Pert, is found in complex molecules called neuropeptides. The brain contains about sixty different neuropeptides, including endorphins. These neuropeptides are the means by which all cells in the body communicate with each other. This includes brain-to-brain messages, brain-to-body messages, body-to-body messages, and body-to-brain messages. Individual cells, including brain cells, immune cells, and other body cells, have receptor sites for these neuropeptides. The kinds of neuropeptides available to cells are constantly changing, reflecting variations in your emotions throughout the day. The kind and number of emotion-linked neuropeptides available at receptor sites of cells influence your probability of staying well or getting sick.

To put it simply, Candace said, "The chemicals that are running our body and our brain are the same chemicals that are *involved in emotion. And that says to me that "we'd better pay more attention to emotions with respect to health. Under the influence of contraction, our cells begin to function inefficiently."*

Viruses use these same receptors to enter into a cell, and depending on how much of the natural peptide for that receptor is around, the virus will have an easier or harder time getting into the cell.

The emotional charge resulting from the accumulation of NEC is blocking the receptor sites of your cells from receiving the message to upkeep basic functions. They can no longer perform the routine tasks of producing proteins that carry out the basic tasks of keeping the body in a perfect state of health. It isn't that disease and imbalance are created by our cells, but rather in the absence of balance, disease and imbalance are created and experienced. Even with a "strict," "proper," or "ideal" diet, nutrients can no longer be assimilated efficiently into the body. This is an interesting fact since so much emphasis has been placed on the importance of diet and exercise as the keys to eliminating and preventing toxicity in the body.

In many alternative practices, there has always been a credibility and acceptance of the common link between the repressed emotion and where in the body the imbalance or disease begins to manifest. According to Oriental medicine, each organ or gland has one or more emotions that influence it. More often than not, the emotional trauma begins to manifest the imbalance in a corresponding organ or gland.

With all this ancient wisdom and modern scientific research as supporting evidence, we can no longer ignore the fact that emotional toxicity plays an equal and perhaps a more dominant role in achieving optimal health.

Cellular memory release is a focused method on accessing and transforming this emotional toxicity, thereby allowing all holistic parts—spiritual, emotional, and cellular—to communicate and regain a state of balance.

The body can be healed only if mind and spirit are also treated. It is very important to access the totality of information.

How the Memory in the Cells Affects Our Perception

(The illustration below is reprinted with permission.)

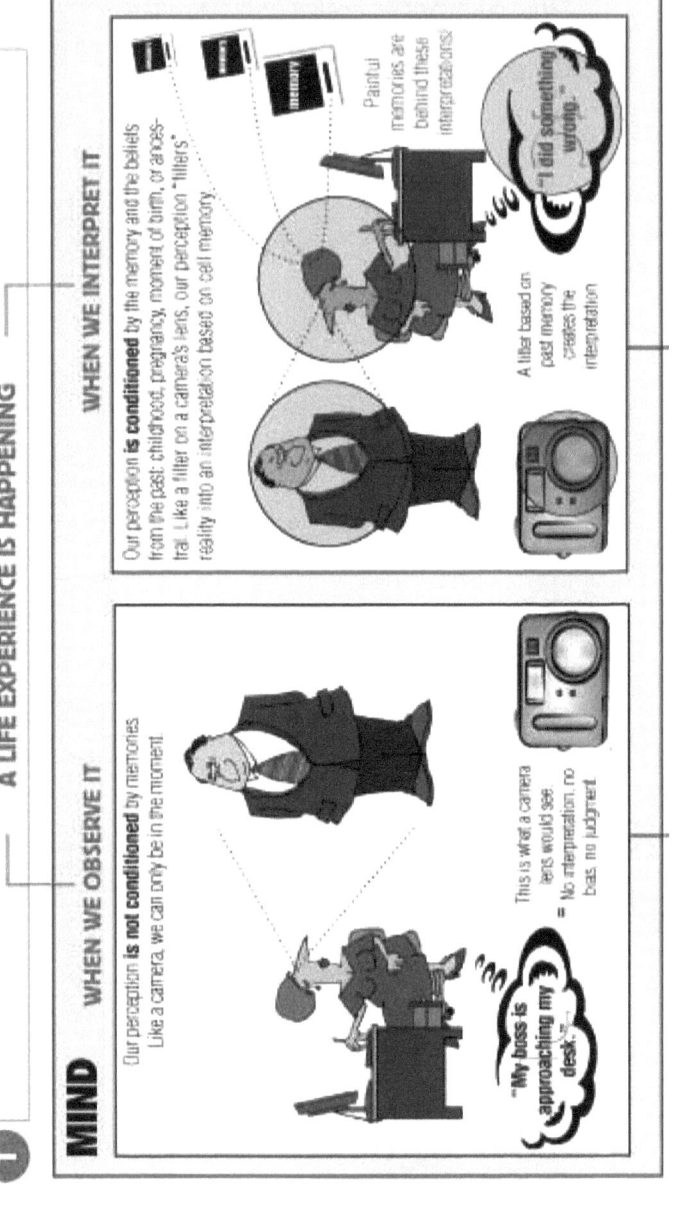

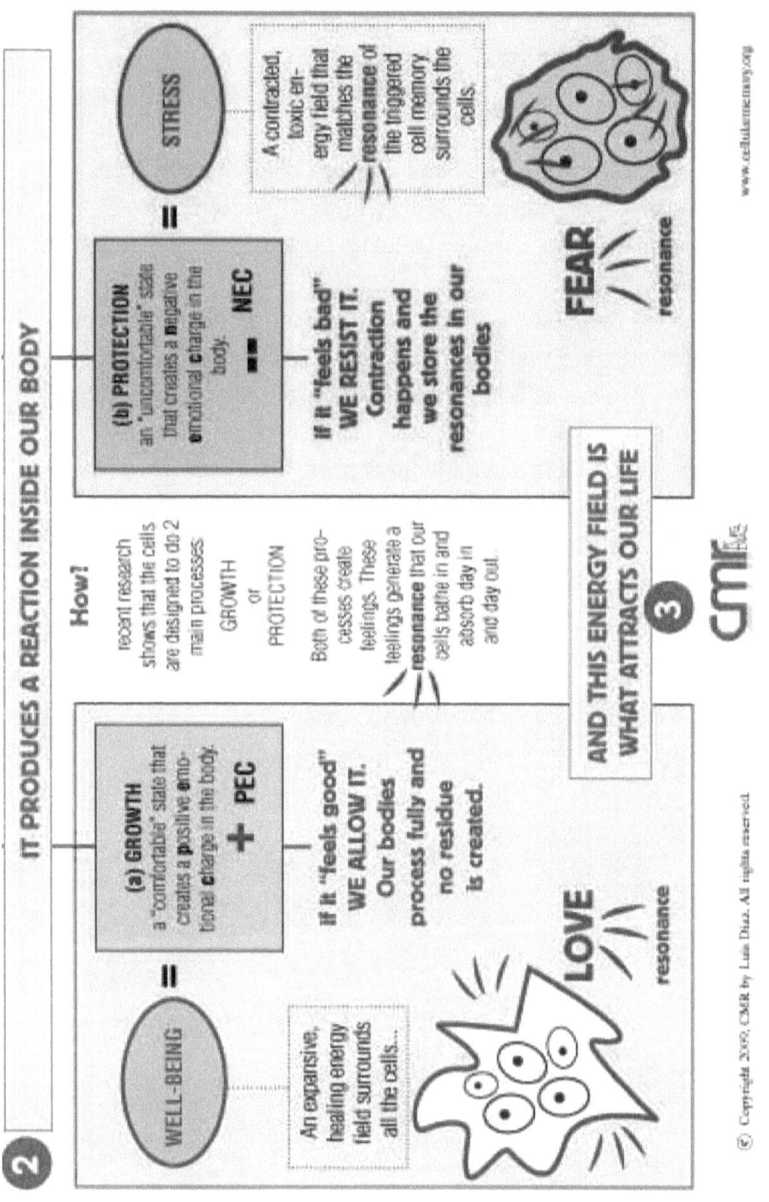

77 American College for Advancement in Medicine, http://www.acam
    net.org/site/c.ltJWJ4MPIwE/b.5470451/k.F16A/ACAM_is_the_
    Voice_of_Integrative_Medicine.htm

78 Cell Talk, John E. Upledger, DO, OMM, pp. 450–451, North Atlantic
    books 2003

79 For more information on Sound Therapy Using Tuning Forks see:
    www.innersoundonline.com or www.ardinwilken.com

80 International Sound Therapy Training Manual 2002, p. 6, ; Sect 2,
    pp. 26–27

81 Destructive Emotions: How Can We Overcome Them? A Scientific
    Dialogue with the Dalai Lama Narrated by Daniel Goleman (pp. 334–
    346); The Benefits of Meditation, Psychology today, (April 1, 2003)
    Colin Allen;

82 Growing the Brain through Meditation, On The Brain: The Harvard
    Mahoney Neuroscience Institute Letter, Fall 2006, Vol. 12 No. 3

83 Primal Panacea 2011 by Thomas E. Levy, MD, JD, p. 37

84 Memory in the Cells – How to change behavioral patterns and release
    the pain body by Luis Angel Diaz 2010 – Additional info on Cellular
    Memory Release can be found at www.cellularmemory.org.

CHAPTER 4

POLITICS—THE ART OF THE POSSIBLE— BE IT GOOD OR EVIL

Where love rules, there is no will to power; and where power predominates, there love is lacking. The one is the shadow of the other.[85]

Rational Discussions

Rational discussions between the political Left and Right are pretty much nonexistent. Both appear to believe it is acceptable to force their will on all. Combined with the Patriot Act, the National Defense Authorization Act, various spy programs, and rewarding Wall Street bankers for defrauding the people, Congress has essentially issued a divorce decree from the people and the principles the United States was founded upon. Their shared view that the rich and powerful should be pampered while their abuses are denied, covered up, excused, and then justified presents the greatest obstacle to meaningful reform, along with all the rules and regulations they make for others while exempting themselves. Profits, power, and greed have largely shut out the voices of the common people, while those who do manage to raise issues are routinely demeaned and dismissed outright. A lack of political knowledge, especially by some on the Left, seems to be one of the reasons America has been on a downward spiral, while the demand for ignorance from the Right is another.

Political Terms

The political terms *liberal, conservative, middle of the road, radical,* and *reactionary* come from the French Chamber of Deputies in the years preceding the French Revolution. The deputies sat in an arc with radicals sitting together on the Far Left. Liberals sat next to them, a little closer to the center with those in center position and not having any strong leanings either way. Conservatives sat just to the right of center and reactionaries on the Far Right. Those on the Left believed a change in the status quo was necessary, while those on the Right fought for the way things were.

Radicals argued for an immediate change, while liberals were in favor of a slow but steady change to improve the welfare of citizens who complained of oppression by the French monarchy. Conservatives were occasionally open to minor changes, but wanted to keep their power and position secure. Reactionaries wanted no change at all. They were wealthy and powerful and believed their wealth and power was a sign from God that they and they alone were fit to rule. All others just existed to obey them. The reactionaries won, and the French Revolution followed. Many reactionaries were imprisoned and beheaded along with King Louis XVI and Marie Antoinette before the tide turned, and those on the Far Left were imprisoned and beheaded. Many in or near the center also met a similar fate.

The French Revolution with all its bloodshed served as a warning against extreme positions and the dangers of extreme wealth in the hands of a powerful few. The lessons of the French Revolution seem to have been lost in the latter part of the twentieth century, continuing to the present time. Many high school textbooks eliminated the role played by reactionaries from the causes of the French Revolution. I believe this started with the state of Texas. As Texas ordered a lot of textbooks, companies found it more profitable to eliminate the role of reactionaries from all textbooks, and most states, including Nevada, went along with it, helping to dumb students down.

Libertarians were perhaps the first to notice that the political dynamic had changed, recognizing the dangers inherent with the concentration of power both in the communist and fascist worlds, and presented a political grid quite different from that of the French Chamber of Deputies. Here is their political grid.

R S BENNETT

WHERE DO YOU STAND POLITICALLY?
To find out, take the world-famous...

World's Smallest Political Quiz

For years, politics has been represented as a choice between left (or liberal) and right (or conservative). Growing numbers of thinkers agree this is far too narrow a view — and excludes millions of people. The political map on the Quiz gives a much more accurate representation of the true, diverse political world. **The Quiz measures *tendencies*, not absolutes.** Your score shows who most agrees with you in politics, and where you agree and disagree with other political philosophies.

——Scoring: For each statement, circle A if you Agree, M for Maybe (or don't know), or D if you Disagree.——

How do you stand on
PERSONAL ISSUES?

	20	10	0
● Government should not censor speech, press, media or Internet.	A	M	D
● Military service should be voluntary. There should be no draft.	A	M	D
● There should be no laws regarding sex between consenting adults.	A	M	D
● Repeal laws prohibiting adult possession and use of drugs.	A	M	D
● There should be no National ID card.	A	M	D

SCORING 20 for every A, 10 for every M, and 0 for every D: _____

How do you stand on
ECONOMIC ISSUES?

	20	10	0
● End "corporate welfare." No government handouts to business.	A	M	D
● End government barriers to international free trade.	A	M	D
● Let people control their own retirement: privatize Social Security.	A	M	D
● Replace government welfare with private charity.	A	M	D
● Cut taxes and government spending by 50% or more.	A	M	D

SCORING 20 for every A, 10 for every M, and 0 for every D: _____

●NOW FIND YOUR PLACE ON THE CHART!

Mark your **PERSONAL** score on the lower-left scale; your **ECONOMIC** score on the lower-right. Then follow the grid lines until they meet at your political position. The Chart shows the political group that agrees with you most.

●WHAT DOES YOUR SCORE ON THE CHART MEAN?

LIBERTARIANS support a great deal of liberty and freedom of choice in both personal and economic matters. They believe government's only purpose is to protect people from coercion and violence. They value individual responsibility, and tolerate economic and social diversity.

LEFT-LIBERALS generally embrace freedom of choice in personal matters, but support central decision-making in economics. They want the government to help the disadvantaged in the name of fairness. Leftists tolerate social diversity, but work for what they might describe as "economic equality."

RIGHT-CONSERVATIVES favor freedom of choice on economic issues, but want official standards in personal matters.

They tend to support the free market, but frequently want the government to defend the community from what they see as threats to morality or to the traditional family structure.

CENTRISTS favor selective government intervention and emphasize what they commonly describe as "practical solutions" to current problems. They tend to keep an open mind on political issues. Many centrists feel that government serves as a check on excessive liberty.

STATISTS want government to have a great deal of control over individuals and society. They support centralized planning, and often doubt whether liberty and freedom of choice are practical options. At the very bottom of the chart, left-authoritarians are usually called socialists, while right-authoritarians are generally called fascists.

Advocates for Self-Government
269 Market Place Blvd., #106 ● Cartersville, GA 30121-2235
800-932-1776 ● Email: Quiz@TheAdvocates.org
Fax: 770-386-8373 ● Web: www.TheAdvocates.org

82

The grid designed by libertarians recognizes the overlapping of reactionaries and radicals. Both are desirous of a powerful central government controlled by them and dictating to the people. While Republicans claim they want a smaller central government, over the past several decades, they have voted to increase the power and control their corporate masters have demanded. They also typically overlook the vast military, which they claim is needed to preserve the American way of life, as well as the huge spy apparatus created to divert attention from the underlying reasons behind the decline of American power. The corporate cloud of indifference toward the welfare of any but the most powerful has contributed to the American way of life, coming to signify a mean-spirited, bullying presence to many.

Central Intelligence Agency (CIA) involvement in the overthrow of various governments in the Middle East, Latin America, and elsewhere show the truth to the criticism. The number of people in state and federal prisons who were never allowed to present a defense is another sign of a growing totalitarianism in America, which increasingly despises freedom.

One criticism of the grid is that it ignores the concerns of environmentalists who recognize our dependency upon other forms of life, both plant and animal, and view loss of natural habitat for them, along with pollution, rising sea levels, ocean warming, waste, ocean acidification, and increased atmospheric CO_2, as the greatest threat to humanity. Perhaps soon, someone will devise a grid that takes these concerns into account.

Classical Liberalism

Classical liberalism is a philosophy committed to the ideal of limited government and liberty of individuals, including freedom of religion, speech, press, assembly, and free markets. Much of the current Left leadership appears to be mainly committed to installing a bureaucratic dictatorship, limiting the rights of individuals, including speech, the press, the right to trial, and the right of the people to peacefully assemble. Privileged parochial urbanites (PPUs) who cannot see past their burkas of money cannot conceive of listening to anyone who isn't in 100% agreement with their agenda. They are seemingly bent on setting up a *patrón* system of government modeled on Tammany Hall, or the Hague machine where favors are currency, intermediaries are needed to conduct any form of business, rights are nonexistent, and people are pawns to be taken advantage of.

Their followers, primarily naive individuals, have been spoon-fed propaganda for so long, they believe it to be the truth. Those who have been enmeshed in liberal organizations for so long have failed to see the trap they have put themselves in. Believing money solves all problems and being overly concerned with the superficial, the Left has ignored the various underlying causes of social problems. While championing the causes of some, they scapegoat others. Their calls for more laws and a larger bureaucracy to hide behind have created additional problems while solving few or none.

Trying to find goodness in the lesser of two evils is
like looking for a rainbow in the rear of a cave.[86]

80/20 Rule of Marketing

Various intrusive government programs have been endorsed by both Left and Right. While they may offer short-term protection to the wealthiest, they are incompatible with a free nation or world. The 80/20 rule of marketing is derived from the broader Pareto principle concept introduced by Italian economist Vilfredo Pareto in 1906. Pareto noted that the majority of wealth in a free market economy is concentrated within a relatively small group of people, roughly 20% of the population. This principle has since been applied not only in business but in politics and government.

Now that more than 80% of the wealth in the United States is in the hands of less than 20% of the population, revolution and political unrest are almost certain. It is likely that unemployment insurance, disability payments, food stamps, and other assistance program work to prevent popular uprisings. According to Professor G. William Domhoff from the sociology department of University of California at Santa Cruz, in the United States 20% of the people own 89% of the wealth, leaving only 11% of the wealth for the bottom 80%.[87] Much of Wall Street seem eager to install a dictatorship in the United States—and throughout the world—with them ruling.

The Community

> The "community" never gave anyone anything. The "community," the "society," the "nation" is just a number of interacting individuals, not a mystic entity floating in the clouds above them. And when some individual— parent, teacher, customer—"gives" something to someone else, it is not an act of charity but a trade for value received in return.[88]

The community is much more than just interacting individuals. Without the planet revolving around the sun within certain parameters, life would not exist—no trees, no grass, no drinkable water, no insects, no bees, no flowers, no mammals, no sea life, no humans. Humans have formed societies that are designed to serve all so individuals and groups see it is in their common interest not to kill others, not to steal, etc. No, we are not perfect, but generally we have been willing to give up certain things for the benefit of the larger group. We all do benefit when the community, the society, or the nation acts with fairness toward all. We all suffer when fairness fades and the strong take unfair advantage of the weak. Yes, most are willing to overlook some advantages the strong take, but not when it consistently threatens the lives and freedoms of the less powerful. The weak then band together and rid themselves of the abuser, no matter how powerful. It is simply natural law. It has been happening for millennia. It is simply cause and effect.

Wall Street has become abusive. It is largely responsible for poisoning streams and rivers, cutting down forests, polluting the oceans, and changing the ratios of oxygen, carbon dioxide, and other gases in the atmosphere, which has resulted in killing off fish and other creatures not part of the economic community but upon whom the human community depends. We need clean air, clean water, food, and shelter, as well as leisure time and community with others. Wall Street has supported invading other countries and driving others into poverty to increase its profits. Wall Street has given misery to millions in exchange for the billions in profits they have made—hardly a trade for value received. By threatening the lives and well-being of many, they are inviting others to threaten the very existence of financial exchanges. Isn't that a part of what Al-Qaida is all about? Isn't it the opposite of the teachings of all religions?

The popular perception is that 80% of Congress spends 80% of its time kissing up to Wall Street, allowing the street to dictate to it, rubber-stamping the bills they want into be laws while deluding themselves that they are simply doing the will of the people. Apparently having mistaken the rectums of Wall Street bankers for the face of God, most in Congress seem to be more than a just a little bit misguided. Moral of the story - if you spend enough time butt kissing to curry favor, you too can be mistaken for a piece of crap.

A free market? Baloney, there must be thousands of laws sponsored by Democrats and Republicans that have exemptions or other provisions for the privileged class to gain some advantage. No wonder so many are looking forward to a total economic collapse. They feel that way things may get back to an equal footing. Perspective is important. A person on the north side of the railroad tracks sees things differently than the engineer driving the train west down the tracks, who sees things differently than a person on the south side of the tracks. Each of them sees things differently than the person walking west along the tracks who has just bent down to tie his shoe.

> *Motesharrei's report says that all societal collapses over the past 5,000 years have involved both "the stretching of resources due to the strain placed on the ecological carrying capacity" and "the economic stratification of society into Elites [rich] and Masses (or "Commoners") [poor]." This "Elite" population restricts the flow of resources accessible to the "Masses," accumulating a surplus for themselves that is high enough to strain natural resources. Eventually this situation will inevitably result in the destruction of society.*
>
> *Elite power, the report suggests, will buffer "detrimental effects of the environmental collapse until much later than the Commoners," allowing the privileged to "continue 'business as usual' despite the impending catastrophe."[89]*

Joe Kennedy, father of President Kennedy, made his first fortune as a bootlegger, primarily bringing booze in from Canada. He made another fortune manipulating the stock market. President Roosevelt appointed him to clean up the corruption on Wall Street, and wanting his family to become respectable, Kennedy did. Having helped create some of the corruption, he knew the ins and outs. Restoring greed and corruption on Wall Street has been the result of close-minded policies that celebrate and ennoble greed. While greed may challenge every generation, the current generation faces the possibility of being wiped out on a massive scale due to greed.

> *From the 1980s onwards, the financial and banking sectors pumped millions of dollars into undoing regulations put in place after the stock market crash and Great Depression of the 1930s. Deregulation has had two major ramifications: corporate executives associated with the banking and*

> *financial sectors have become exceptionally wealthy, and*
> *global markets have become much more risky, culminating*
> *in the global economic crisis that began in 2008. . . . there*
> *is a direct correlation between financial deregulation and*
> *economic inequality in the US.*[90]

Fleecing the sheeple and then sending them off to slaughter or be slaughtered in wars are among the ways Wall Street prospers.

The Wealthy Have Often Prospered from Wars

The wealthy have often prospered from wars and revolutions. The French Revolution and communist takeover in Russia were exceptions. "The time to buy is when there's blood in the streets" is more than just a saying on Wall Street; it is an affirmation that those on Wall Street are willing to create chaos and misery in order to obtain greater profits for a select few. The financial crisis of the past several years is just an example of their willingness to defraud and blame the less well-off for the problems they created. That the Democrats rewarded them for their duplicity is just a sign that the Democrats have abandoned the people and become the party of lawyers, bureaucrats, and Wall Street profiteers. As Republicans can be considered point guards for Wall Street, they offer little of value for those with limited financial resources.

Meanwhile, the bureaucratic darlings of the Left produce seemingly endless rules and regulations for the people they are supposed to serve to follow. Perhaps nowhere else is this more evident than in the mental health systems the various states have set up. The excesses due to overregulation have been ignored, and abuses justified. Currying favor with the powerful has been on the rise, promoted by much of the media and seemingly endorsed by many on the Left and Right, as well as in many schools.

California even has a state law that elevates those who mastered this skill to the top when the state hires, although it likely wasn't the laws intention. Those who are able to maintain an A average in college when they receive a bachelor's degree are put on the top of the list when it comes to hiring in state government. While this is seemingly a reward for hard work, the reality is often quite different. Many professors talk about students who parrot back exactly what they say in class, or otherwise try to curry favor, but are unable to have a serious conversation about the topics raised in class. Many of these same students defer at all times to the professor's point of view even when the point of the exchange is to challenge the students to arrive at their own conclusions. While this strategy doesn't work well in science and math classes, in many liberal arts classes it is enough for some students to achieve an A, obtain a high-paying government job, and expect others to then kiss up to them.

Conservatives

Conservatives have been fighting "godless" communism for so long that they have ignored their own core principles. The religious Right, in its erroneous claim that America was founded to be a Christian nation, seems to be ignorant both of history and the teachings of Christ.

The abuse of power by religious authorities has a long history in Europe (and the Middle East) and contributed to the rise of communism in Russia, the French Revolution, and other abuses. When people use religion to excuse coercion, intimidation, hatred, and violence, religion becomes just another word for intolerance. Of course, much of what is considered to be the excesses of religion were merely abuses by the most powerful in the name of religion. Most in the hierarchy of the church came from the families of the nobles and identified with the concerns of the nobles over that of the common people. "Treat others as you would like to be treated" is a primary teaching of Christ.

Too often it has been ignored by those claiming to be Christians. Those who advocate violence, hate, or revenge are not Christians. None of these are part of the New Testament.

Censored

I wanted to insert an ad by the Republican Party in the 1950s that showed the support Republicans had for labor unions, which cited the great prosperity the nation had at the time, as well as support for social security, good pay for workers, good working conditions, and more, and I asked readers to imagine the ad being run now. However, I have been informed that copyright laws prevent my doing this. Some claim that current copyright laws can often work to censor material that is needed for thoughtful discussions. Liberty—parent of science and industry, as our nation once proclaimed—is seriously threatened.

Those who call themselves conservatives today spend much time utilizing Schopenhauer's thirty-eight unethical ways to win an argument to silence those who disagree even a little. If they would remove their heads from their soiled sandboxes, drop their demagoguery, and spend time listening to average citizens, they could win over many who fear the Right more than they distrust the Left. As the Left has recently adopted using Schopenhauer's insane tactics, rational discussions have become even more difficult.

Schopenhauer's Thirty-Eight (Unethical) Ways to Win an Argument

These ways include the following:

- Ignore your opponent's proposition, which was intended to refer to some particular thing. Rather, understand it in some quite different sense, and then refute it. Attack something different than what was asserted.
- Confuse the issue by changing your opponent's words or what he or she seeks to prove.
- Make your opponent angry. An angry person is less capable of using judgment or perceiving where his or her advantage lies.

Any who use these arguments are out to cheat or deceive.

Arthur Schopenhauer (1788–1860) was a German philosopher best known for his book *The World as Will and Representation* (German: *Die Welt als Wille und Vorstellung*), in which he claimed that our world is driven by a continually dissatisfied will, continually seeking satisfaction. See appendix for all thirty-eight ways.

The American Conservative Union

The following highlighted statements were adopted in December 1964 by the American Conservative Union. The commentary is mine.

> *We believe that the Constitution of the United States is the best political charter yet created by men for governing themselves. It is our belief that the Constitution is designed*

to guarantee the free exercise of the inherent rights of the individual through strictly limiting the power of government.

I agree with this statement.

We reaffirm our belief in the Declaration of Independence, and in particular the belief that our inherent rights are endowed by the Creator. We further believe that our liberties can remain secure only if government is so limited that it cannot infringe upon those rights.

I agree with this, although I have semantic quibbles with the phrase "the Creator" as I consider the creation as synonymous with God.

We believe that capitalism is the only economic system of our time that is compatible with political liberty. It has not only brought a higher standard of living to a greater number of people than any other economic system in the history of mankind; more important, it has been a decisive instrument in preserving freedom through maintaining private control of economic power and thus limiting the power of government.

Capitalism has perverted itself by ignoring or discarding some basic rules of economics. Considering the increasing numbers of people in this nation who are in prison, lack housing, or are unemployed, as well as the increased concentration of wealth in the hands of a few, it is time to step back, drop the hardened positions, and have rational discussions aimed at solving the various underlying problems. More about this below and in the chapter on economics.

We believe that collectivism and capitalism are incompatible, and that when government competes with capitalism, it jeopardizes the natural economic growth of our society and the well-being and freedom of the citizenry.

I disagree. There has always been a mix of collectivism and capitalism in the nation. The United States was formed under mercantilism. While mercantilism and capitalism are related, labor has value in mercantilism. The armed forces are a form of collectivism as is Congress, citizen groups, the bureaucracies, police forces, fraternal organizations, Girl and Boy Scouts, churches, and any time people band together for the common good. Government needs to regulate financial markets in order to prevent them from becoming abusive of the public welfare. Should government own nonvoting stock in corporations, it may be possible to eliminate income and other taxes.

> *We believe that it is the responsibility of the individual citizen, whenever his inherent rights are threatened from within or without, to join together with other individuals to protect these rights, or, when they have been temporarily lost, to regain them.*

I agree.

> *We believe that any responsible conservative organization must conduct itself within the framework of the Constitution; in pursuance of this belief we refuse to countenance any actions which conflict in any way with the traditions of the American political system.*

I agree.

> *Capitalism leads to dole queues, the scramble for markets, and war. Collectivism leads to concentration camps, leader worship, and war.*[91]

Economic growth does have its limits. Its growth can become, or rather, has become cancerous. Other types of growth, such as personal growth, spiritual growth, and the growth of wisdom need to be considered as well. At least one modest change to the current version of capitalism has been offered by economic geographer David Harvey, who claims that while capitalism has been very important and productive, it also requires a 3% growth factor forever, and this is not sustainable. The large amounts of capital in the hands of a relative few cannot find enough creative production to invest in and has turned to schemes to make money from money, such as derivatives, bundling high-risk loans together while claiming they are low-risk, and other deceptive practices. This and other possible solutions need to be discussed.

Various environmental facts, such as the acidification of the oceans, the millions of people living on $2 or less a day, peak human population expected to be between nine and twelve billion by 2050, and other crises, demand serious conversations about making the world a better place for all who inhabit it. "Kissing up to the rich and powerful" may well become the new national motto if we continue the way we are going.

Inclined to Liberty: A Geographic Perspective

Libertarians are generally fond of the book *Inclined to Liberty: The Futile Attempt to Suppress the Human Spirit* by Louis E. Carabini. I looked forward to reading it after receiving a copy following the debate between President Obama and Governor Romney, which I viewed at the University of Nevada, Reno. A talk given by libertarian VP candidate Judge Jim Gray was part of the program. The book starts with how people fall into one of two competing categories: (a) those who are inclined toward liberty and the freedom of the individual to live life as he or she sees fit, as long as they are peaceful, and (b) those who are inclined to mastery and want to permit others to exist only in a manner in which they, the masters, see fit. Yet much of the book is about how righteous it is that corporations should have mastery over individuals. The Borg of Star Trek is apparently the author's desired form of civilization.

Inclined to Liberty is a book that forces the reader to think. Arriving at one's own conclusions, thinking for oneself, is unfortunately frowned upon in some political, educational, and governmental circles. What I thought was going to be an enlightening read was at times a difficult chore. Often I arrived at different conclusions from the author, despite having some areas of agreement.

I do agree that government exercises too much control over the lives of individuals and this often puts individuals in positions that can be difficult to escape from. However, corporations do the same thing. Those who have mastered themselves have no need to control others, favoring liberty for all. But liberty requires being responsible for one's actions and being willing to lend a helping hand. We are all connected, and each of us, from time to time, requires a hand from others. The more people, as well as corporations and governments, take responsibly for their actions and the consequences of those actions, the more liberty and freedom can be enjoyed by all.

"It is not fair that companies can terminate workers just to increase profits." This is the first of many arguments/statements in the book that can give rise to thoughtful discussion. The book essentially argues that corporations have no obligation to their workers. Companies are formed to make a profit, but the belief that they should also benefit the larger community has been the underlying reason they have been encouraged to exist, at least until the last couple of decades. When corporations become a net burden to communities, they should be encouraged to leave.

When corporations do need to terminate employees, how and why it is done helps determine how rocky a road the company will face in the future. Fair notice, possibly with help offered to find workers other employment, will foster good relations and have former employees feel good about the company that once employed them. When it is done with callous disregard for the lives and welfare of the employee and their families, it will breed discontent. This can create even greater problems for the company if and when former employees, or their allies, obtain some position where they can exert some measure of control over the company's future.

Should the workers share in these profits, or should they be disposed of as soon as possible if an avenue to make even greater profits arises?

The answer the author gives is that it is fair that workers should be terminated with little or no notice. At first glance it would seem that the business owners are rather stupid. Closing down an existing profitable business just so they can invest their money elsewhere seems kind of dumb as they could sell the business to the employees who enjoy the work.

A more provocative and thoughtful answer, however, is given by the Twelve Visions Party (TVP), which believes current corporations and newly formed companies should be formed or reformed along lines that reward individuals/employees according to the value they add to the product or revenue line. This would provide incentive to employees to continue to give their best, have nonsales positions help generate sales, and avoid burnout while increasing loyalty and profits. While the owners would wind up with a smaller percentage of revenue, they would gain in actual dollars.

TVP incorporates many of the values of libertarians but contains a substantial amount of propaganda as well, believing no company would ever do anything that would ever cause harm to any. Having grown up in New Jersey, between the Hackensack and Hudson Rivers, I was aware from an early age that both corporations and government would often abuse their power. The Hackensack River was considered a dead river where fish were unable to live, and it would catch fire on a regular basis due to all the wastes the chemical companies dumped into it. Looking out over the Hudson, one could regularly see barges of garbage that had been set on fire. This was a method New York considered proper for disposal despite the fact that much of it often wound up on the Jersey side.

Unfortunately, to my way of thinking, the value added sharing methodology would likely begin to break down when a company grows beyond fifteen to twenty employees, although it could possibly work until two hundred to two hundred fifty people worked for the organization. Still I believe this portion of TVP should be endorsed by every small business, and the difficulties dealt with as they present themselves. After all, a nation of small businesspeople and those working for small businesses has many advantages, including a greater inclination to help the local community, which among other things should cut down on the need for taxes.

The Twelve Visions of the Twelve Visions Party

1. Be the person you were meant to be.

2. Live the life you were meant to live every day.

3. Feel extraordinary every day.

4. Slow down aging permanently.

5. Land the job of your dreams.

6. Build the business of your passion.

7. Experience the love of your life.

8. Have the body you always envied.

9. Become a genius of society.

10. Have everything you ever wanted (via the free-to-soar geniuses and super technologies).

11. Ride a prosperity wave to riches (via falling prices and soaring buying power).

12. Enjoy nearly perfect health (via soaring medical technologies and falling prices).

I believe TVP offers value to voters, but their hyperbole and repetition essentially amounts to little more than brainwashing, while their authoritarian leanings will chase others away. With some seasoning and a willingness to hear out their critics, TVP could become a force in American politics.

Often, when huge corporations come into a community, they become not a benefit to the community but a net liability. Some receive tax abatements so they aren't required to support schools, libraries, parks, police, or pay their share of salaries to other city workers. The burden gets shifted to existing companies or individuals. The increased competition forces some existing businesses to lay off workers—or even close their doors. These smaller companies then cut back on the amount of time or money that they donate to the community. This results in fewer uniforms for Little League, less time volunteering at the Girl Scouts, fewer donations to the homeless shelter, and a general worsening of conditions for those affected. The pay employees of these huge corporations receive can often be less than required to maintain a decent home and acquire meals and clothing for the employee and his or her family. Some employees become eligible for benefits from taxpayers. The lawyers and other con artists who arranged for the tax abatement get their pay, however. Tax abatements for huge corporations harm local communities as the money they would otherwise have paid into making life better for all goes into the pockets of Wall Street robber barons. As long as Congress maintains, as they seemingly do, the attitude that the people exist to worship corporate behind, problems will grow larger in this nation.

Malthus

Malthus wrote *An Essay on the Principle of Population* in 1798 and in doing so provided a spur to the development of the technology, which increased crop production and influenced the opening of new and marginal land for crops. Some of the political leaders at the time strove to solve the problems Malthus addressed. Without this thoughtful essay, they would have been ignorant of various problems that were on the horizon. According to *Inclined to Liberty*, Malthus was and is wrong and essentially should be ignored. Technology will always provide an answer, and population growth is not a problem. With a huge garbage spiral in the Pacific Ocean, a large portion of the Gulf of Mexico considered a dead zone due to the runoffs of chemical fertilizer used in agriculture, and Monsanto's GMO crops, the solution technology often now presents is death.

World population is expected to rise from the current seven billion people worldwide to nine (some estimate twelve) billion by 2050 before leveling off, with the greatest population increases occurring in the developing world.[92] This increases the risk of famine, war, and other deprivations. In *Beyond Malthus: Sixteen Dimensions of the Population Problem*, the authors lay out the various problems and presented partial solutions in diverse areas, a sort of geographical compendium (grain production, fresh water, biodiversity, climate change, oceanic fish catch, jobs, cropland, forests, housing, energy, urbanization, natural recreation areas, education, waste, meat production, and income). These problems resulted not just from the rise in population but the technology that Malthus's essay helped to spawn, as well as the human inclination toward greed and indifference.

While the percentage of the US population aged five to nineteen will decrease from 20.3% in 2010 to 19.2% in 2050, their numbers are expected to rise from sixty-three million in 2010 to nearly eighty-five million by 2050.[93] Schools need to be reorganized to adequately meet the current and approaching challenges. Gardening needs to become a topic of study—not just book learning but actually growing food that can be used for school lunches or taken home by students who will hopefully start home gardens. Courses on economics, rational thinking, and emotional intelligence should be given starting in junior high or perhaps sooner. There is a need to encourage people to use both sides of their brain. Science and art both need to be encouraged. Schools should also present information on managing one's emotions, including anger. There is also a need for more skilled workers, including the manual arts. Engineers, electricians, carpenters, welders, metalworkers, and others, such as those trained in the healing arts, will always be needed. We have too many engaged in the manipulation of finances, emotions, and information, which produce nothing of real value.

There are stresses upon the planet that threaten much of life on earth, including the various structures we all depend upon to varying degrees. While I am confident that life on earth will endure, humans may not—those who live closest to the earth have the best chance of survival. It will take intelligent effort to maintain an adequate living for all. The more living standards decline, the greater is the risk for all, including stable governments. Increased harmony among the peoples of the nation and the world is needed to achieve this. People are dependent upon the earth and her resources; the earth is not dependent upon the people.

The many advances in science made during the past century should not be ignored. Many of these advances will allow us to meet the challenges that lie ahead, but the law of unintended consequences should not be ignored. Ignoring problems will neither make them go away nor diminish them.

The ability to recognize trauma symptoms should also be required of teachers. Those who live with the effects of trauma are frequently not able to make rational decisions. These include a good many students. Economic realities require greater reliance on individuals and families. We cannot continue to support a huge bureaucracy, especially when that bureaucracy does not give value for tax dollars—and we certainly do not need more government scolds.

Debt is a form of slavery. For thirty years or more, both Democrats and Republicans have been urging Americans to take on more debt for the sake of "the economy." Yet the benefits of "the economy" have gone to Wall Street bankers and others dedicated to the pursuit of power and greed. Congress, the White House, and the various bureaucracies are all in the hands of those who have been advocating for the American people to become slaves of a corporate empire where privileges for the rich are increased while rights for the individual are diminished. America has had its dream hijacked by the quest for ever-growing corporate and bureaucratic power.

85   Carl Jung - *The Psychology of the Unconscious*, 1943

86   The Secret Way of Wonder by Guy Finley Pg. 90

87   Who Rules America, Wealth, Income, and Power, by G. William Domhoff, http://www2.ucsc.edu/whorulesamerica/power/wealth.html

88   Give Back? Yes, it is time for the 99% to give back to the 1%, by Harry Binswanger, Forbes Sept. 17, 2013; http://www.forbes.com/sites/harrybinswanger/2013/09/17/give-back-yes-its-time-for-the-99-to-give-back-to-the-1/

89   NASA Study Concludes When Civilization Will End, And It's Not Looking Good for Us http://mic.com/articles/85541/nasa-study-concludes-when-civilization-will-end-and-it-s-not-looking-good-for-us

90   WORKING FOR THE FEW, Political capture and economic inequality p. 12

91   George Orwell, *The Observer*, 9 April 1944- Review of *The Road to Serfdom* by F. A. Hayek and *The Mirror of the Past* by K. Zilliacus,

92   *Beyond Malthus: Sixteen Dimensions of the Population Problem, WorldWatch, 1998*

93   US Census Bureau, Statistical Abstracts of the States: 2012, table 9 Resident Population Projections by sex and age: 2010-2050.

CHAPTER 5

A SHORT COURSE ON ECONOMICS

True individual freedom cannot exist without economic security and independence. People who are hungry and out of a job are the stuff of which dictatorships are made. [94]

The Six Fundamentals of Economics

(This chapter is primarily based on the course *Thinking Like an Economist: A Guide to Rational Decision Making* by Professor Randall Bartlett of the Smith College, the Teaching Company.)

1. People respond to incentives. Disincentives do nothing to promote certain activities.
2. There is no such thing as a free lunch: Everything has at least an opportunity cost even if it doesn't have a monetary cost. If you are doing one thing, you won't be able to do something different at the same time. If you take a walk in the park, you can't be at work at the same time, unless of course, you work in the park, take a smartphone with you, or are an artist/writer. While modern technology may seem to muddy this fundamental, the basic premise remains valid.
3. No thing is just one thing. Everything is connected; there are two or more sides to every interaction. Every

sale requires a purchase and often a pickup or delivery. A glass of water is not just glass and water; it exists due to rain, rivers, the pipes that bring the water to the faucet, those who made and shipped the glass to the store where it was purchased, and much more.

4. There are unanticipated influences. Be it adverse weather closing a road or someone whispering in your ear, there are unanticipated circumstances that can influence results.

5. Law of unintended consequences: actions, once taken, can and will have consequences that were not intended. Some of these may be favorable, others unfavorable. Some will be slight, some massive, others moderate. This cannot be avoided despite how much one plans. Actions should generally be limited in scope to reduce unintended consequences. Endlessly long and complicated regulations merely cause greater problems and confusion while increasing costs for attorneys. At times the confusion appears to be deliberate, inserted for the benefit of attorneys who expected to be hired to solve the impasses they helped to create.

6. No one is in control. No matter how much skill or power you, your team, or computer has, other forces are at play. While failing to skillfully exert enough power or energy may result in something not being implemented, too much force can also destroy even the best intended project . . . or nation.

Core Concepts in Economics

Marginal Analysis

How much is a little more of something worth? Typically things happen gradually, a little more of this, a little less of that. Each additional thing is less valuable than the preceding item. The value of a glass of water varies depending on circumstances. It has a small value when a person is sitting next to a faucet that can easily be turned on yet a completely different value if that same person has been stranded in the desert for days. However, when things change radically, marginal analysis becomes less meaningful.

How much is a little more or a little less government worth? Have we reached a tipping point where *a little more* government will thrust us into a bureaucratic dictatorship where decisions are made solely to provide short-term benefits for those in its employ? Or will anarchy be the result?

In any voluntary, well-informed exchange, both parties can win because they are trading one thing that has two different values. Value in transactions is judged *on the margins*—slight improvements in the well-being of the parties. In marginal analysis it is assumed that rational individuals will voluntary enter any transaction that makes them better off. If all the participants are made better off, it's a Pareto improvement.[95]

Marginal analysis does demonstrate that the multimillion dollar salaries and bonuses of corporate CEOs have gone well past the point where the standard of living for these individuals can rise to a higher level. The financial crises created by deceit for the financial benefit of major banking corporations raised unemployment and forced demonstrable decreases in the living standards of many. This sent many into homelessness or onto the couches of friends or family and forced others to sell their homes at less-than-perceived true value. Others chose to stay in their homes but not make any mortgage payments. These individuals typically fared better, sometimes payment-free for years, than renters who would typically face eviction within weeks or months of failing to pay rent.

Rationality

Rationality is a process. Contrary to popular belief, rationality makes no judgment about the wisdom of the objective; it is merely about how we decide to do something. If we are rational we each will chose what we believe to be our own best interest. Beliefs, experience, cultural attitudes, education, mental health, prejudice, ignorance, commitment, skill, and ability all factor into both choosing objectives and the means by which we attempt to achieve them.

Rational deciders won't consent to their own harm. They also won't refuse a clear gain. Incentives must be true, complete, and accurate. It must be recognized, however, that many transactions are not entirely voluntary, nor are the parties always well informed. This is especially true in the criminal justice and mental health systems. In these systems, true incentives often do not exist.

Efficiency

Efficiency evaluates the social consequences—the consequences of all rational decisions.

According to a physicist, efficiency is achieving a given amount of work with a minimum amount of energy. According to an economist, efficiency is making people as well-off as they can be, given the resources available. The Pareto optimum situation is when no one can be made better off without harming another. It is considered an increase in efficiency. People are being harmed to increase the portfolio wealth of a few. Our economy has become increasingly inefficient as a result.

The 80/20 rule of marketing is basically this: Ignore the bottom 80% of the population and concentrate on the top 20%. This top 20% provides 50% of sales. Then ignore 80% of the top 20%—which leaves only the top 4%, which provides 25% of all sales. In other words, 80/20 is an infinite repeating *fractal* pattern. This means very tiny causes produce huge effects. This makes great sense from a marketing or sales perspective but a disaster from a social perspective. Marketing has also moved from finding needs that can be met, which has been a cause of strength in the capitalist system, to promoting whatever makes the most money for the wealthiest. Broad-based innovations then languish and systems begin to collapse. Advertising has become more about brainwashing than informing people about ways to fulfill needs and wants.

What happens to the bottom 80% of the people and then, to a lesser extent, to all but the top 4%? Concentration of benefits for the top percentage means the lower 80% are poorly served. Eventually a tipping point will occur when those at the bottom revolt, especially when the top few percent have no qualms about killing, starving, imprisoning, enslaving, or drugging them because they are considered a waste of time and resources. *Useless eaters* was a term used by Nazi Germany to scapegoat the disabled, the homosexuals, the political dissidents, the Roma, and the Jews they blamed for their loss of political and economic power, including hyperinflation, in the years following World War I.

Optimization

The best or optimal outcome. If something makes one person better off by their own judgment without making anyone worse off, then that is a social improvement. Accordingly, the Pareto optimum situation is when no one can be made better off without harming another. It doesn't mean it's just, fair, or ideal; it is just efficient. We have fallen far from the Pareto optimum. Neither Wall Street nor governments can decide when an individual is better or worse off. Only the individual can do that.

Balancing Short and Long Term

One difficulty is balancing short- and long-term considerations of the few versus the many. On a global scale, this is being played out by those who are concerned about the future due to policies and actions that have resulted in acidifying of the oceans, global warming, rising ocean levels, the dying of many species, and other serious environmental issues. Environmentalists typically desire policies that would have positive long-term impacts, such as solar power and reduced usage of coal and oil, with a willingness to forgo policies that, while producing huge short-term benefits for a few, have a huge negative long-term effect on everyone. Naturally, those who have gained the most financially from coal, oil, and pollution have been opposed to anything that could threaten their dominance. With Washington, DC, and Sacramento poised to be under water,[96] literally and not just financially by 2150, perhaps a few more politicians will start to understand that keeping their heads in the sandbox does not yield good results. Long term in nature is not six months as currently considered by the financial world. Neither ruled, frightened, nor impressed by money, the forces of nature will not bend to the highest bidder. Blackmailing God or nature is not a tactic than can end well for anyone.

Another difficulty the Western mind-set has is in understanding cultures where the payoff may be in a form other than money or other types of immediate material gratification. People value various incentives, money just being one of numerous possible payoffs. Incentives can include increased free time, happiness both short and long term, comfort, friendship, quality of life, increased harmony, diversity, and appreciation of other forms of existence, including differing species. In corporate and governmental circles, spirituality, religion, and environmental concerns are sometimes considered just a form of delusion to be derided when they are not being manipulated for economic gain.

What is best for one group may not be best for others or the whole; it can even be harmful. Lack of balance in laws and policies can create political dissent, which can lead radical change, be it violent or not. Prior to political plans being implemented, all affected need to be informed and consulted, free from coercive interference. Failure to do so can result in dire unintended consequences. Much of the poverty in America today can be traced to political and economic actions that have rammed certain actions down the throats of the people so a favored few could benefit. The war on poverty, while well intended, is such a case. Typically, those who stand to gain the most financially also have long histories of giving large campaign contributions to political candidates. It is much easier to side with what is most beneficial for the rich and powerful than it is to act rationally in the best interest of all.

While money may be a measurement of success, it is by no means the best standard. Perceived fairness is a better standard. Many in the top echelons of government and the corporate world appear to believe they are immune to the laws of physics. These laws, including that of cause and effect, apply in the human realm as well as in the scientific realm. Neither Wall Street, Congress, the president, nor the Supreme Court has the ability to overrule them. Humans do have the ability to manipulate energy, including the energy that is latent in the stocks and bonds of Wall Street. However, chaos becomes more likely when significant shifts are imposed to force significant redistributions of energy or wealth. Many currently believe chaos is now inevitable given Wall Street's grip on nearly every facet of life.

> *Worldwide the 85 richest people own the same amount as the bottom half of the entire global population. The ramifications of such inequality may be dire.*[97]

> *According to Credit Suisse, 10 percent of the global population holds 86 percent of all the assets in the world,*

while the poorest 70 percent (more than 3 billion adults) hold just 3 percent.[98]

400 of the richest Americans have more wealth than the 150 million citizens who comprise the poorest half of the population.[99]

Concentration of wealth in the hands of the few leads to undue political influence, which ultimately robs citizens of natural resource revenues, produces unfair tax policies and encourages corrupt practices, and challenges the regulatory powers of governments. Taken together, all of these consequences serve to worsen accountability and social inclusion [100]

Redistributions of Wealth

The biggest redistributions of wealth have been from the people and small businesses to Wall Street and the various government bureaucracies. This latest redistribution was deliberately created by Wall Street bankers to transfer wealth from the people to the bankers. Many would prefer to simply enjoy the diverse wonders of the world rather than spend a lifetime squeezing money from everything and everyone. Life is a grand university and lessons can be found in the strangest places.

A concern about having more women in Congress is that the women who do enter politics tend to come from the upper income brackets and have no real knowledge of actual conditions for those in lower income brackets. However, the same can be said of the men entering politics, yet greater female representation can bring wider perspectives to problem solving.

Many at various economic levels seem to agree that those on Wall Street have simply become power-crazed perverts who have succeeded in reaching the somewhat dubious goal of being rich and powerful enough that they can bribe Congress into making their unethical actions legal—even willing to bankrupt the nation to do so.[101]

> *You will observe with concern how long a useful truth may be known, and exist, before it is received and acted upon.*[102]

[94] President Roosevelt, January 11, 1944 State of the Union Address

[95] Economist Vilfredo Pareto 1848–1923

[96] Study: global warming related sea level rise poses big threat to Washington, DC., By Andrew Freedman. Washington Post Jan 17, 2012 http://www.washingtonpost.com/blogs/capital-weather-gang/post/study-global-warming-related-sea-level-rise-poses-big-threat-to-washington-dc/2012/01/16/gIQAlMGb5P_blog.html: Which US City Will Be the First Submerged by Climate Change? http://news.yahoo.com/u-city-first-submerged-climate-change-234941462.html;_ylt=A0SO8wEYYVFUSYUAgg5XNyoA;_yl u=X3oDMTEzbDRuZmFjBHNlYwNzcgRwb3MDNARjb2xvA2dxM QR2dGlkA1ZJUDIyN18x

[97] There Are 85 People Who Are As Wealthy As Half The WORLD, Oxfam Reports http://www.huffingtonpost.com/2014/01/21/85-richest-people_n_4641021.html

[98] WORKING FOR THE FEW, Political capture and economic inequality http://www.oxfam.org/sites/www.oxfam.org/files/bp-working-for-few-political-capture-economic-inequality-200114-en.pdf, p. 50

[99] Ibid., p. 22

[100] Ibid., p. 11

[101] *US politics' true bipartisan consensus: capitalism is untouchable* by *Richard Wolff, Chair of the Council of Economic Advisors in the Economy Branch of the Green Shadow Cabinet*

[102] Letter to Benjamin Vaughan by Benjamin Franklin, July 31,1786

CHAPTER 6

TOWARD THE DARK SIDE—
SUPREME COURT DECISIONS

*The due administration of justice is the
firmest pillar of good government.*[103]

Constitutional Rationality

The US Supreme Court rules on the constitutional rationality,
not on the wisdom or the likely consequences of the decisions it
makes. Then there are the unavoidable unintended consequences.
It is the duty of the other two branches of government to act
as checks and balances when one of the three branches causes
abuses to occur. However, in order to understand when these
abuses are occurring, it is necessary to listen to the people.
Yes, the people are not all smooth and polished and at times
can be difficult to understand. However, politics is the art of the
possible, and perhaps this book can begin an awakening and
remind the three branches of government to respect and listen
to all the people, not just to the polished lobbyists on Capitol
Hill who spread around huge cash contributions. Indeed, these
same lobbyists may be financially benefitting from the abuses
that others are being forced to endure. The entire Constitution,
including the preamble, needs to be respected.

> *We the People of the United States, in Order to form a more perfect Union, establish Justice, insure domestic Tranquility, provide for the common defence, promote the general Welfare, and secure the Blessings of Liberty to ourselves and our Posterity, do ordain and establish this Constitution for the United States of America.*

Having encountered a number of abuses during my arrests from both police and attorneys, including an unwillingness of either to hear me out or permit me to come to trial where I would be allowed to make my case, I came to the conclusion that there were deep-seated systemic problems that needed to be addressed. While it has taken me more than twenty years to come to my conclusions, much too late to have them heard in court, I now take them to the people, who I hope will make their representatives take the time to listen. I try to cover what I see as the major issues. I am fairly certain that there are other unaddressed matters as well.

The Prisoners' Dilemma

The *prisoners' dilemma*[104] is an economic game theory well-known to police, prosecutors, and to a lesser extent, those accused of crimes. It has major flaws, including the assumption of guilt and working to cover up police errors and misconduct. It has also decayed the self-correcting mechanisms—appeals and challenges to unwise or unjust laws and severely limiting public involvement by largely doing away with trials. The prisoners' dilemma is a pressure cooker that has made a farce out of a once well-respected system, although noting that certain segments of the population have historically been denied due process. The number of people imprisoned, primarily for nonviolent crimes, is obscene: 2.2 million,[105] plus another 3.94 million on probation and 851,000 on parole as of 2012.[106] Supreme Court decisions have helped set America on the path to the dark side.

In its purest form, the prisoners' dilemma occurs when two or more individuals are held and the authorities believe they have committed one crime and are suspected of another. The prisoners are held apart from one another and offered a deal. The first one who confesses to both crimes is given a lighter sentence than he would have received for the one crime for which there is strong evidence. The remaining suspects will then face a harsher penalty than the early confessor.

Some will confess early at times, implicating individuals who either weren't involved in any crime or sometimes rival gang members. Implicating someone who was involved can result in revenge being extracted against the early confessor or his or her family. Refusing to cooperate helps to form and strengthen ties to street gangs. The prisoners' dilemma also strengthens the code of silence within police departments, which also is a negative for the community. We have record number of inmates[107] but few convicts. The system has earned the distrust of the people.

> *Evil ... defined most simply as the use of political power to destroy others for the purpose of defending or preserving the integrity of one's sick self.*[108]

Miranda v. Arizona

A vicious cycle began with the implementation of the plea bargain system. The utilization of the prisoners' dilemma began as a prosecutorial response[109] to *Miranda v. Arizona* (384 US 436, 1966). In this decision, most well-known for having police read a suspect their rights, also mandated that everyone facing six months imprisonment—which includes misdemeanors in possibly every state—or longer is entitled to an attorney, and if the accused cannot pay for it, that it will be paid for by the county in which the crime was committed. As the cost for attorneys increased expenses for every county in America, an alternative to the justice system was sought without any input from the public, and the plea bargain system was hatched while truth, fairness, and justice were thrown out the window. In some states, including Nevada, it is only a one day difference of possible imprisonment between an attorney being required or not. The greatest abuses in the system are typically found in large metropolitan areas.

Among the unintended consequences of *Miranda*[110] are the following:

A. Police rarely give suspects an opportunity to clear themselves.

B. More suspects are arrested.

C. Plea bargains have largely replaced trials.

D. Crime is encouraged and rewarded.

E. The innocent and those with mitigating circumstances are often scapegoated.

F. Police errors and abuses are often covered up.

Waiving time, lawyer shorthand for giving up the right to a fair and speedy trial, is commonplace. When I asked my attorney what it meant, he said it was to delay a trial for a few days so he could get ready. A few days turned out to be thirty days, and then he just pressured me to plead no contest. When I tried to enlist his aid to obtain prescription medication for a medical condition I had since age eleven, he told me "That's what all you people use as an excuse" before turning and walking away. This same attorney also refused my request to read a copy of the police report.

Due to this, in 1988 I was forced to make the choice between dying in the Los Angeles County Jail or pleading no contest to misdemeanor charges I did not believe myself guilty of. This occurred on the seventy-third day of solitary confinement.[111] I had been denied access to pen, pencil, paper, telephone, and prescription medication. The California Bar Association did not see anything wrong with the actions of the attorney. I was released from the jail on Bastille Day, July 14, only to be rearrested the next day on the charge they had lost me for the second time.

The actions of my various attorneys did vary, and not all performed each of the following actions. However, in general the performance consisted of the following:

1. Upon meeting, tell defendant, "Plead no contest and I can get you out of jail by tomorrow."
2. Should defendant protest innocence, tell defendant, "It doesn't make any difference if you are guilty or not, plead no contest anyway. That's the way the system works."
3. Should defendant still protest, display contempt toward defendant with a physical gesture, which I described in *Mental Illness: A Guide to Recovery* as the Los Angeles county salute. Most frequently this would involve attorneys and others in positions of authority turning and giving an exaggerated wiggling of the buttocks to the defendant. Once I had an attorney spread his rear cheeks at me. This occurred following an arrest on a warrant issued in the wrong name. It took more than a month before I could get anyone to check my fingerprints. I then received a judicial clearance[112] on those charges. However, the failure by the county of Los Angeles to remove the wrongful charges from my record for several years likely contributed to other arrests.
4. Should defendant still protest, inform defendant that charges will be increased and that he will not receive any assistance from the attorneys and will spend years in prison, even if only charged with a misdemeanor. Some attorneys were very open about helping police cover up abuses.

I have had defense attorneys tell me, "We [the attorneys] decided to protect the public by seeing to it that everyone charged with a crime will be found guilty of something" and "if you were innocent, you would have been born rich enough to afford a good attorney."

The above described actions generally took place not in the courtroom but in the conferences that occur prior to the proceedings that are closed to all except attorneys and defendants. These conferences can be crowded with defendants resulting in extreme lack of privacy. Other defendants often overhear everything spoken, including threats and misinformation from the attorneys.

The conviction rate in Los Angeles, according to *The Criminal Justice Profile*, published by the State of California, rose from 81% in 1981 to 98.6% in 1988, when most of my arrests occurred, and falling only to 96% in 1996. This coincided with the use of plea bargains, previously considered unethical by most attorneys for not just major crimes but misdemeanors as well. California discontinued publishing this informative guide after the 1996 edition in an apparent attempt to cover up the abuses in their justice system.

> *The right to trial lies at the heart of America's criminal justice system. Yet trials have become all too rare in the United States because nine out of ten federal and state criminal defendants now end their cases by pleading guilty.*[113]

What Is the Responsibility of a Public Defender Toward a Criminal Defendant?

Is it to assist the accused in the preparation of a defense, as stated in the US Constitution, Amendment VI or not? "In all criminal prosecutions, the accused shall enjoy the right to a speedy and public trial; by an impartial jury of the State and district wherein the crime shall have been committed, which district shall have been previously ascertained by law, and to be informed of the nature and cause of the accusation; to be confronted with the witnesses against him; to have compulsory process for obtaining witnesses in his favor, and to have the assistance of counsel for his defense." Many who have gone through the criminal justice system consider most public defenders to be little more than government-paid rectum pointers.

Plea bargains have been encouraged for a variety of reasons:

- The costs and time involved in trials is reduced.
- The ability to have more cases come before a judge is increased.
- They strengthen the political power of the prosecutor.
- They reduce the costs involved in having officers testify while increasing the number of officers on the street.
- They satisfy public demand that something should be done.

While the Nevada Supreme Court has directed public defenders to obtain a statement from defendants prior to offering any plea deal, individuals who have been arrested in Nevada tell me that this doesn't always happen. Other states may not even have this requirement.

A short video, "The Plea Bargain System—An Evil Destroying America?" can be found at http://youtu.be/ VSZZXgevT7k.

US constitutional jurisprudence offers scant protection from prosecutors who are willing to pressure defendants into pleading and punish those who insist on going to trial. Courts do not view defendants as unconstitutionally coerced to forego their right to a trial if they plead guilty to avoid a staggering sentence. Nor do they consider defendants to have been vindictively—that is, unconstitutionally—punished for exercising their right to trial when prosecutors make good on their threats to seek much higher mandatory penalties for them because they refused to plead. Finally, even when courts agree that prosecutors have sought egregiously long mandatory sentences for drug offenses, they will not rule the sentences so disproportionate as to be unconstitutionally cruel.[114]

Punishment to Fit the Crime?

Under well-established criminal justice principles, reflected in US and international human rights law, convicted criminal offenders should receive a punishment commensurate with their crime and culpability and no longer than necessary to serve the legitimate purposes of punishment. Those purposes include holding offenders accountable for their wrongdoing, protecting the public by keeping them in prison, deterring crime, and rehabilitating the offenders. They do not include penalizing defendants for going to trial or discouraging future defendants from doing so.

Prosecutors nonetheless believe a defendant's insistence on going to trial is a perfectly legitimate reason to pursue an increased sentence—even one that is wholly disproportionate to the underlying offense. As a former US Attorney told us: "We weren't trained to think about the lowest sentence that serves the goals of punishment."[115]

Even prosecutors who try to achieve fair sentences through plea bargains acknowledge that the quest for fairness ends if the defendant refuses to plead. Prosecutors also insist they are not "punishing" defendants with higher sentences when they refuse to plead guilty, but rather "rewarding" defendants who, by pleading, spare them the expenditure of time and resources needed for a trial. From the perspective of the defendant looking at a significant trial penalty, this is no distinction.

Once they have made a threat during plea negotiations, prosecutors believe they must follow through with it if the defendant goes to trial, both because a defendant who refuses to plead deserves "no mercy," and because they want to be sure future defendants take their threats seriously. They think they will lose credibility if they permit defendants to reap the same sentencing "concessions" after a trial as they had been offered if they pled. Asked if they thought these much higher post-trial sentences are just, prosecutors dodged the question.[116]

Blind belief in authority is the greatest enemy of truth.[117]

Imbler v. Pachtman

In *Imbler v. Pachtman* (424 US 409, 1976), the US Supreme Court encourages malicious and overzealous prosecution, apparently setting prosecutors above the law in callous disregard of the preamble to the Constitution. Much earlier the Supreme Court pointed out that the goal of the sovereign in a criminal prosecution is "not that it shall win a case, but that justice shall be done."[118]

The facts of the *Imbler* case are as follows:

1. He was imprisoned for murder and sentenced to death.
2. After nine years a federal court freed him, citing misleading or false testimony by the prosecution.
3. Imbler filed a lawsuit seeking damages from the prosecutor.
4. The prosecutor, at some time following Imbler's conviction, sent the governor a letter saying newfound evidence cast doubt on the conviction.
5. The Supreme Court ruled that district attorneys or prosecutors to have full immunity from civil suits resulting from their government duties and the ultimate fairness of the operation of the system itself could be weakened by subjecting prosecutors to § 1983 liability.

[A] significant number of innocent defendants are pressured to plead to crimes they did not commit. And within the much larger universe of guilty defendants, those who are punished most severely are often those who

made the worst deals, not those who committed the worst crimes.[119]

Imbler v. Pachtman stands in vivid contrast to *Chisholm v. State of GA* (2 US 419, 1793), which was about a similar matter.

But, the framers of the Constitution could never have thought thus. They must have viewed human rights in their essence, not in their mere form. They had heard, seen—I will say felt; that Legislators were not so far sublimed above other men, as to soar beyond the region of passion. Unfledged as America was in the vices of old Governments, she had some incident to her own new situation: individuals had been victims to the oppression of States.

Then it was the present Constitution produced a new order of things. It derives its origin immediately from the people; and the people individually are, under certain limitations, subject to the legislative, executive, and judicial authorities thereby established. The States are in fact assemblages of these individuals who are liable to process. The limitations, which the Federal Government is admitted to impose upon their powers, are diminutions of sovereignty, at least equal to the making of them defendants.

Let us now turn to the Constitution. The people therein declare, that their design in establishing it, comprehended six objects. 1st. To form a more perfect union. 2nd. To establish justice. 3rd. To ensure domestic tranquility. 4th. To provide for the common defence. 5th. To promote the general welfare. 6th. To secure the blessings of liberty to themselves and their posterity. It would be pleasing and useful to consider and trace the relations which each of these objects bears to the others; [2 US 419, 475] and to show that they collectively comprise every thing requisite, with the blessing of Divine Providence, to render a people prosperous and happy on the present occasion such disquisitions would be unseasonable, because foreign to the subject immediately under consideration.

In February term, 1794, judgment was rendered for the plaintiff, and a writ of enquiry awarded. The writ, however, was not sued out and executed so that this cause and all the other suits against states were swept at once from the records of the Court by Amendment XI to the federal constitution, agreeable to the unanimous determination of the judges, in *Hollingsworth et al. v. Virginia*, argued at February term, 1798.

Amendment XI

How did the Amendment XI to the Constitution factor into justifying malicious prosecutions and having the Supreme Court ignore the preamble to the Constitution? Somehow, the adoption of the Amendment XI to the Constitution eventually helped to set the stage for the court to rule in favor of malicious prosecution of individuals and to ignore the preamble to the Constitution as they were no longer able to consider, as precedence *Chisholm v. State of GA*.

> **AMENDMENT XI**
> *Passed by Congress March 4, 1794. Ratified February 7, 1795.*
> [**Note:** Article III, section 2, of the Constitution was modified by Amendment XI.]
> *The Judicial power of the United States shall not be construed to extend to any suit in law or equity, commenced or prosecuted against one of the United States by Citizens of another State, or by Citizens or Subjects of any Foreign State.*

It is also my understanding that the court no longer considers the preamble when deciding cases. Ignoring intent both of defendants and of the Constitution is, in my opinion, a grave mistake.

William Anderson, in his blog[120] on prosecutorial immunity claims that "a prosecutor knows that he or she does not operate with the same set of personal restrictions that hold back the worst behavior in other occupations. . . . A nation that has Rule of People Who Do whatever They Want cannot survive as a decent society."

Mr. Anderson also mentions in his blog the case of *Pottawattamie County v. McGhee* where prosecutors clearly frame innocent people and then claimed that there is no constitutional "right not to be framed." How many prosecutors believe it is acceptable to frame people?

The following is an excerpt from my earlier book
Mental Illness: A Guide to Recovery:

Some argue ("Win at All Costs," *Pittsburg Post Gazette*, Nov. 22–Dec. 13, 1998) that since the 1976 US Supreme Court decision, *Imbler v. Pachtman* (424 US 409), which held that a prosecutor cannot be held liable for deliberate malicious and dishonest actions that deprive an individual of life or liberty, prosecutors regularly fabricate and hide evidence. The various mandatory sentencing laws imposed by Congress also preclude mitigating circumstances from being considered in sentencing.

The plea bargain system is designed to suppress the truth. The public typically believes prosecutors when they whine about defendants who outwit the system. Savvy defendants can abuse the system, but it is only because the system has become perverted, becoming more an instrument to deny justice that these abuses thrive.

Public defenders are typically no more than lackeys of the prosecutor. They are good little messenger boys and girls. The first time a defendant meets the public defender assigned to him, he is told the length of the sentence that will be given in exchange for a no contest plea.

Currently the fairness of the justice system is being questioned due to prosecutorial misconduct, Supreme Court decisions, mandatory sentencing laws, get-tough-on-crime laws, zero-tolerance laws, three-strikes laws, prison overcrowding, lack of trials, privatization of prisons, and the millions of incarcerated people and those on parole or probation.

The court has been a factor in the growth of the phony epidemic of mental illness that has gripped the nation. This is due to decisions like *Imbler v. Pachtman*, which significantly go against reason or the administration of justice, and a driving force in the increase in the number of people diagnosed with a mental illness due to the trauma associated with discovering the court is no longer concerned with justice.

If the Supreme Court indeed believes malicious prosecutions are outside the purview of the courts and lie in the hands of the citizens, what should be done? To answer this, at least two questions must be asked and answered.

A. What does "in the hands of citizens" mean?
B. Possible interpretations are the following:
   - By contacting elected representatives
   - By voting
   - By recalling petition
   - By demonstrating
   - By force
     - By police or other authorities
     - By armed citizen groups
C. How is the citizenry becoming aware of malicious and overzealous prosecutions?
   - Juror complaints to justices
   - Media coverage, including news articles and commentaries
   - Citizen attendance at trials
   - Social media

While newspapers covered problems with this decision more than twenty years ago, the media today seems most intent on advancing propaganda that provides greater financial advantage to corporate owners or greater bureaucratic control over the lives of the citizenry. *Imbler v. Pachtman* still cries out for public and congressional debate and action, but ignoring the duty to the citizenry has become the rule rather than the exception.

The status of the media, newspapers, and television has fallen dramatically over the past thirty years in apparent concert with corporate ownership of the press. The Internet is full of conspiracy theories, spam, misinformation, and a few tidbits of useful information hidden here and there. The corporate-owned news media appear to be only interested in propaganda that advances the short-term interest of their corporate masters and loathe to reveal anything that does not advance the corporate agenda. At a public relations seminar I attended, the presenters were absolutely giddy when they told the class that 80% of the content of some newspapers comes exclusively from press releases.

In a very telling article[121] that appeared in the July 15 edition of The New York Times, *Jeremy W. Peters readily admits that most news organizations have become little more than propagandists for the political elite, even going so far as to grant government officials and candidates "veto power" over statements and quotes attributed to them on the printed page.*

"It was difficult to find a news outlet that had not agreed to quote approval, albeit reluctantly," writes Peters. "Organizations like Bloomberg, The Washington Post, Vanity Fair, *Reuters and* The New York Times *have all consented to interviews under such terms."*

In July, veteran news reporter Andrea Seabrook left National Public Radio (NPR) after 14 frustrating years working under similar conditions that exist within the realm of broadcast journalism. During a recent interview[122] with Politico, Seabrook stated: ". . . I feel like

I am, as a reporter in the Capitol, lied to every day, all day. There is so little genuine discussion going on with the reporters. . . . To me, as a reporter, everything is spin."[123]

An Example of Overzealous Prosecution

I worked with a woman for several months after her release from Lake's Crossing, the psychiatric forensic facility in Sparks, Nevada, where she had spent thirteen years. According to her husband, she had gone driving without her glasses, which she very much needed. As he related it, she stopped the car a couple of hundred yards after thinking she hit something and was going back to see what she hit. As it turned out, it was a man, and he was dead. She was arrested.

At some point a psychiatric examination was ordered, and she was found to be incompetent to stand trial and given a diagnosis of schizophrenia. During the hearing, the prosecutor made numerous references to a completely different woman who, years earlier, had driven on the sidewalk, killing six people. After she had been held for between two and three years, her husband had a conversation with her primary doctor, who told him that they had increased her medication several times, and she was considered noncooperative primarily because she refused to admit that she had killed six people.

Her husband then informed the doctor she had only killed one person, not six. Although she is now generally free from the confines of a psychiatric facility, she is not doing all that well. She created an entire family in her mind during the thirteen years of being locked up in the forensic facility, and at times her primary concern is this imaginary family. It is unknown how much the doctor's actions, due to being influenced by an overzealous prosecutor, has been a factor in her inability to adequately recover—or ever come to trial.

Recently, I had a conversation with a psychiatrist who worked with Pricilla Ford, the woman who did drive on the sidewalk in Reno, killing six people and injured another twenty-three on Thanksgiving Day 1980. This was during her last appeal against her death sentence, many years after she had been convicted. Using a PET scan, this psychiatrist was able to find a brain tumor located on the basal ganglia,[124] which was the true cause of aberrant behavior by this former school teacher. Had this test been performed earlier, it is possible a different verdict may have been reached. Pricilla Ford died in prison of natural causes.

Bordenkircher v. Hayes[125]

> *MR. JUSTICE STEWART delivered the opinion of the Court.*
>
> *The question in this case is whether the Due Process Clause of the Fourteenth Amendment is violated when a state prosecutor carries out a threat made during plea negotiations to reindict the accused on more serious charges if he does not plead guilty to the offense with which he was originally charged.*
>
> *The Due Process Clause of the Fourteenth Amendment is not violated when a state prosecutor carries out a threat made during plea negotiations to have the accused reindicted on more serious charges on which he is plainly subject to prosecution if he does not plead guilty to the offense with which he was originally charged. Pp. 434 US 360–365.*
>
> *"[T]he guilty plea and the often concomitant plea bargain are important components of this country's criminal justice system. Properly administered, they can benefit all concerned."*
>
> Blackledge v. Allison, *431 US 63, 431 US 71. Pp. 434 US 361–362*
>
> *(b) Though to punish a person because he has done what the law allows violates due process, see* North Carolina v. Pearce, *395 US 711, 395 US 738, there is no such element of punishment in the "give-and-take" of plea*

bargaining as long as the accused is free to accept or reject the prosecutor's offer. Pp. 434 US 362–364.

This Court has accepted as constitutionally legitimate the simple reality that the prosecutor's interest at the bargaining table is to persuade the defendant to forgo his right to plead not guilty, and, in pursuing that course here, the prosecutor did not exceed constitutional bounds. Pp. 434 US 364–365.

MR JUSTICE BLACKMUN, with whom MR. JUSTICE BRENNAN and MR. JUSTICE MARSHALL join, dissenting.

I feel that the Court, although purporting to rule narrowly (that is, on "the course of conduct engaged in by the prosecutor in this case," ante this page), is departing from, or at least restricting, the principles established in North Carolina v. Pearce, *395 US 711 (1969), and in* Blackledge v. Perry, *417 US 21 (1974). If those decisions are sound and if those principles are salutary, as I must assume they are, they require, in my view, an affirmance, not a reversal, of the judgment of the Court of Appeals in the present case.*

In Pearce, as indeed the Court notes, ante at 434 US 362, it was held that "vindictiveness against a defendant for having successfully attacked his first conviction must play no part in the sentence he receives after a new trial." 395 US at 395 US 725. Accordingly, if, on the new trial, the sentence the defendant receives from the court is greater than that imposed after the first trial, it must be explained by reasons "based upon objective information concerning identifiable conduct on the part of the defendant occurring after the time of the original sentencing proceeding," other than his having pursued the appeal or collateral remedy. Id. At 395 US 726. On the other hand, if the sentence is imposed by the jury and not by the court, if the jury is not aware of the original sentence, and if the second sentence

*is not otherwise shown to be a product of vindictiveness,
Pearce has no application.* Chaffin v. Stynchcombe, *412
US 17 (1973).*

*Then later, in Perry, the Court applied the same
principle to prosecutorial conduct where there was a
"realistic likelihood of vindictiveness."' 417 US at 417 US
27. It held that the requirement of Fourteenth Amendment
due process prevented a prosecutor's reindictment of
a convicted misdemeanant on a felony charge after
the defendant had exercised his right to appeal the
misdemeanor conviction and thus to obtain a trial de
novo. It noted the prosecution's "considerable stake" in
discouraging the appeal.*

*The Court now says, however, that this concern
with vindictiveness is of no import in the present case,
despite the difference between five years in prison and a
life sentence, because we are here concerned with plea
bargaining where there is give-and-take negotiation,
and where, it is said, ante at 434 US 363, "there is no
such element of punishment or retaliation so long as the
accused is free to accept or reject the prosecution's offer."
Yet, in this case, vindictiveness is present to the same
extent as it was thought to be in Pearce and in Perry;
the prosecutor here admitted, see ante at 434 US 358
n. 1, that the sole reason for the new indictment was to
discourage the respondent from exercising his right to
a trial. [Footnote 2/1] Even had such an admission not
been made, when plea negotiations, conducted in the
face of the less serious charge under the first indictment,
fail, charging by a second indictment a more serious
crime for the same conduct creates "a strong inference"
of vindictiveness. As then Judge McCree aptly observed,
in writing for a unanimous panel of the Sixth Circuit, the
prosecutor initially "makes a discretionary determination
that the interests of the state are served by not seeking
more serious charges."* Hayes v. Cowan, *547 F.2d 42, 44*

(1976). I therefore do not understand why, as in Pearce, due process does not require that the prosecution justify its action on some basis other than discouraging respondent from the exercise of his right to a trial.

Prosecutorial vindictiveness, it seems to me, in the present narrow context, is the fact against which the Due Process Clause ought to protect. I perceive little difference between vindictiveness after what the Court describes, ante at 434 US 362, as the exercise of a "legal right to attack his original conviction," and vindictiveness in the "give-and-take negotiation common in plea bargaining.'" Prosecutorial vindictiveness in any context is still prosecutorial vindictiveness. The Due Process Clause should protect an accused against it, however it asserts itself. The Court of Appeals rightly so held, and I would affirm the judgment.

[Footnote 2/2]

. . .

Second, it is healthful to keep charging practices visible to the general public, so that political bodies can judge whether the policy being followed is a fair one. Visibility is enhanced if the prosecutor is required to lay his cards on the table with an indictment of public record at the beginning of the bargaining process, rather than making use of unrecorded verbal warnings of more serious indictments yet to come.

Finally, I would question whether it is fair to pressure defendants to plead guilty by threat of reindictment on an enhanced charge for the same conduct when the defendant has no way of knowing whether the prosecutor would indeed be entitled to bring him to trial on the enhanced charge. Here, though there is no dispute that respondent met the then-current definition of a habitual offender under Kentucky law, it is conceivable that a properly instructed Kentucky grand jury, in response to the same considerations that ultimately moved the Kentucky Legislature to amend the habitual offender statute, would have refused to subject respondent to such an onerous penalty for his forgery charge. There is no indication in the record that, once the new indictment was obtained, respondent was given another chance to plead guilty to the forged check charge in exchange for a five-year sentence.

MR. JUSTICE POWELL, dissenting.

. . . Respondent was charged with the uttering of a single forged check in the amount of $88.30. Under Kentucky law, this offense was punishable by a prison term of from 2 to 10 years, apparently without regard to the amount of the forgery. During the course of plea bargaining, the prosecutor offered respondent a sentence of five years in consideration of a guilty plea. I observe, at this point, that five years in prison for the offense charged hardly could be characterized as a generous offer. Apparently respondent viewed the offer in this light and declined to accept it; he protested that he was innocent, and insisted on going to trial. Respondent adhered to this position even when the prosecutor advised that he would seek a new indictment under the State's Habitual Criminal Act which would subject respondent, if convicted, to a mandatory life sentence because of two prior felony convictions.

. . . yet the addition of a conviction on a charge involving $88.30 subjected respondent to a mandatory sentence of imprisonment for life. [Footnote 3/1] Persons convicted of rape and murder often are not punished so severely.

No explanation appears in the record for the prosecutor's decision to escalate the charge against respondent other than respondent's refusal to plead guilty. The prosecutor has conceded that his purpose was to discourage respondent's assertion of constitutional rights, and the majority accepts this characterization of events. See ante at 434 US 358 n. 1, 434 US 364.

It seems to me that the question to be asked under the circumstances is whether the prosecutor reasonably might have charged respondent under the Habitual Criminal Act in the first place. The deference that courts properly accord the exercise of a prosecutor's discretion perhaps would foreclose judicial criticism if the prosecutor originally had sought an indictment under that Act, as unreasonable as it would have seemed. [Footnote 3/2] But here the prosecutor evidently made a reasonable, responsible judgment not to subject an individual to a mandatory life sentence when his only new offense had societal implications as limited as those accompanying the uttering of a single $88 forged check and when the circumstances of his prior convictions confirmed the inappropriateness of applying the habitual criminal statute. [Footnote 3/3] I think it may be inferred that the prosecutor himself deemed it unreasonable and not in the public interest to put this defendant in jeopardy of a sentence of life imprisonment.

Perhaps too many Supreme Court justices have been unduly influenced by their time as prosecutors and have too rarely seen things from the other side of the bench. All too often, individuals are threatened with enhanced sentences to cover up abuses of police. While I was willing to fight misdemeanor charges of disturbing the peace which originated due to a seizure—in part to bring to light actions of officers who strapped me to a bed and took turns kicking me, breaking my shoulder—when the prosecutor threatened to increase the charges to a felony for which five years in prison could result, and the public defender told me that they would not be willing to offer me any help whatsoever, I capitulated and plead no contest, receiving summary probation. I had only served about an hour in jail before my shoulder was broken after which I was transported to a hospital from which I was released following surgery. The officers told me following breaking my shoulder that "they were teaching me a lesson."

Frazier v. Cupp

The United States Supreme Court in *Frazier v. Cupp* (394 US 731, 739, 1969) ruled that the police can lie in order to extract a confession. Officers may lie to obtain evidence, they are permitted to fabricate evidence, and they may lie and tell a suspect that a murdered person is still alive or a living person is dead. The only place an officer cannot tell a falsehood is while testifying under oath in court, and criminal defense attorneys occasionally catch officers lying, even on the witness stand. While a seldom-used lie can work to prevent death or injury, the more officers lie, the less police in general will be believed or trusted. Many individuals have come to the conclusion that if it is acceptable for authorities to lie to and mislead them, it is also acceptable for them to lie to police and other authorities.

Salinas v. Texas

In *Salinas v. Texas* (570 US ___ 2013) the United States Supreme Court ruled (5–4) that persons who are not under arrest must specifically invoke their Amendment V privilege against self-incrimination in order to avoid having their refusal to answer police questions used against them in a subsequent criminal trial. This decision is a chilling reduction in individual rights and brings the United States one step closer to being a police state. There is a difference between coerced speech, free speech, and anticipatory speech where one is expected to speak with authority on events that have not yet and may never transpire—which is what SCOTUS seems to require of possible defendants in this decision.

"What today's ruling by the Supreme Court says, essentially, is that citizens had better know what their rights are and understand when those rights are being violated, because the government is no longer going to be held responsible for informing you of those rights before violating them," said constitutional attorney John W. Whitehead, author of A Government of Wolves: The Emerging American Police State. *"Mind you, this is the same court that agreed that cops who tasered a pregnant woman couldn't be held accountable because they were not aware that repeated electro-shocks qualified as constitutionally excessive and unreasonable force."*[126]

Mutual Pharmaceutical Co. Inc. v. Bartlett[127]

In this case, in which a prescription drug was found to have caused an acute case of toxic epidermal necrolysis, which resulted in the respondent becoming severely disfigured, developing physical disabilities, and becoming nearly blind, it was ruled that state laws that conflict with federal law are "without effect" and that it would be impossible for Mutual to comply with both its federal-law duty not to alter sulindac's label or composition and its state-law duty to either strengthen the warnings on sulindac's label or change sulindac's design, leaving Bartlett without legal recourse for injuries suffered. At the time of the prescription, the label's warnings did not specifically refer to toxic epidermal necrolysis.

The primary problem with this decision, as I see it, is the court's unwillingness to adequately address a source of conflicts between federal and state laws—the overreach of the regulatory power of the bureaucracies, particularly the Food and Drug Administration, which much of the public sees as nothing but a rubber stamp for drug companies.

Cherokee Nation v. Georgia[128]

The Cherokee Nation asked for an injunction, claiming that Georgia's state legislation had created laws that "go directly to annihilate the Cherokees as a political society." The court did hear the case but declined to rule on the merits. While Georgia argued that the Cherokee are aliens, not owing allegiance to the United States, the court determined that the framers of the Constitution did not really consider the Indian tribes as foreign nations but more as "domestic dependent nation[s]," and consequently the Cherokee Nation lacked the standing to sue as a "foreign" nation. While the court stated the Cherokee were "acknowledged to have an unquestionable, and heretofore unquestioned right to the lands they occupy, until that right shall be extinguished by a voluntary cession to our government," President Jackson essentially ignored it, resulting in the expulsion of the Cherokee Nation. Their relocation and route is called the Trail of Tears. Of the fifteen thousand who left, four thousand died on the journey to "Indian territory" in the present-day state of Oklahoma.

Factors That Need to Be Considered

Citizens United v. Fed. Election Commission (558 US 310), which allows corporations to give unlimited funds to political parties, needs to be discussed and debated. As far as I can tell, this decision appears to assume that Congress is above the influence of money and the power of wealth. Our Congress has always been influenced by money and power. We have human beings in Congress, as well as in the executive branch, the bureaucracies, and even on the Supreme Court. Human beings are fallible; this includes those who sit on the high court.

My research into trauma helped me better understand why various things were happening in my life. Essentially, an individual may place himself (or others) in harm's way due to an unconscious effort to achieve a better outcome of a traumatic experience. My first arrest occurred when I approached a police car for help in getting to my doctor, and I was charged with assaulting officers who believed I was on drugs. As I recollect the event, as I approached the police car, an officer exited from the passenger side of the police car and began assaulting me with a nightstick as I bent down to speak to the officer who was driving. The last time I was arrested ended with my appointed attorney being fired or at least forced to resign and the charge against me being dismissed. Having a better outcome (the attorney being fired or forced to resign) helped enable me to move on. While both charges involved abusive behavior by officers, either Los Angeles police or sheriff's deputies, I am not aware of any disciplinary action taken against any of them. In responding to a letter from the Sheriff's office I received the day charges were dismissed against me due to the deputies inability to appear in court, I included a copy of the defense I had prepared, which outlined the actions the deputy had initiated against me, part of an initiation procedure to intimidate other sheriff deputies, which included an assault against me, as well as filing false charges.

As I understand it, any deputy who reported the incident to higher ups would find other officers would fail to respond in a timely manner should that deputy put in a call for assistance. Not only had similar things been reported on T.V. and in the newspapers some ten years earlier, but at that time a deputy sheriff friend of mine had told me that two of his friends had been hospitalized when their call for assistance had gone unheeded. He also told me that he was next on the list.

> *Research indicates that on any given day more than seven million children may have a parent in prison or jail, or under parole or probation supervision. Children of incarcerated parents are at risk of poor school performance, drug use and mental health problems, and more likely to be exposed to parental substance abuse, extreme poverty, and domestic violence. Unfortunately, connecting these children to services can be difficult for government agencies, and*

little is known about their specific needs or how effectively these needs are being addressed.[129]

Trauma and its effects, as well as the various nondrug treatments currently available, need to be taken into consideration by the courts. Additionally, the laws and court decisions that work to silence individuals need to be reevaluated not just by the courts but by legislative bodies, as well as in newspapers and other media.

Mental health courts, which help individuals get housing and treatment so they don't spend their lives in jail, prison, hospitals, and the streets due to circumstances that overwhelm them, are a step in the right direction, but more is needed to be done to reduce or eliminate the various circumstances that contribute to pushing people over the edge. The various Supreme Court decisions presented, combined with laws, policies, and procedures in Los Angeles and possibly elsewhere, have been a major factor in distrust of authorities. The fears raised by urban elites too often take too shallow a look at the various problems they seek to address and use emotionally laden arguments to force quick change—which unfortunately often work to create greater problems. All too often narrowly focused experts, who often have economic ties to the solutions they present, are called up to offer their opinion of what needs to be done, and evidence and solutions from less vocal sources and economic-disinterested sources are ignored. Currently those who push for greater gun control laws seem completely unaware of the conflicts being generated by previous court decisions and the abuses that have resulted, including a nation that has been increasingly arming itself. An atmosphere of distrust permeates America. The difference between respect for authority and having authority imposed on the people is something Congress, the Supreme Court, the executive branch, the media, and the people need to review, lest we extinguish ourselves as a free and democratic republic.

We have met the enemy . . . and he is us.[130]

[103] Letter to Edmond Randolph from George Washington on September 28, four days after signing the Judiciary Act of 1789

[104] *Thinking Like an Economist – A Guide to Rational Decision Making* by Professor Randall Bartlett, Smith College, The Teaching Company

[105] "The US penal population of 2.2 million adults is the largest in the world." The Growth of Incarceration in the United States: Exploring Causes and Consequences 20104 National Academy of Sciences, p.2

[106] The Growth of Incarceration in the United States: Exploring Causes and Consequences 2014 National Academy of Sciences. pp. 40–41

[107] America has around 5% of the world's population, and 25% of its prisoners. Roughly one in every 107 American adults is behind bars, a rate nearly five times that of Britain, seven times that of France and 24 times that of India. . Why does America have such a big prison population? Aug 14th 2013, The Economist http://www.economist.com/blogs/economist-explains/2013/08/economist-explains-8

[108] People of the Lie; The Hope for Healing Human Evil by M. Scott Peck, MD (p. 241)

[109] Justice Denied, Len Downie Jr., 1973

[110] Note – These will vary from county to county, and may not be uniform within counties.

[111] It has been more than 20 years since I counted back, and it is possible that the 73 days includes the arrest five to ten days prior. After several days' imprisonment, I was released without being brought to court; and unknown to me a warrant had been issued for my arrest. After being assaulted by an officer (which the Chief of Police in Long Beach apologized for years later) I was arrested again.

[112] *Judicial clearance 26367*

[113] *An Offer You Can't Refuse How US Federal Prosecutors Force Drug Defendants to Plead Guilty* p. 1, 2013 Human Rights Watch

[114] An Offer You Can't Refuse How US Federal Prosecutors Force Drug Defendants to Plead Guilty, p. 3

[115] Ibid., *Human Rights Watch telephone interview with former US Attorney (name withheld), April 25, 2013.*

[116] An Offer You Can't Refuse, pp. 6–7

117 Albert Einstein, Einstein: His Life and Universe by Walter Isaacson 2008

118 Berger v. United States. 295 US 78, 88 (1935).

119 William J. Stuntz, The Collapse of American Criminal Justice (Cambridge: Harvard University Press, 2011), p. 58.

120 http://williamlanderson.blogspot.com/2011/03/how-far-should-prosecutorial-immunity.html

121 http://www.nytimes.com/2012/07/16/us/politics/latest-word-on-the-campaign-trail-i-take-it-back.html?pagewanted=all

122 http://www.politico.com/news/stories/0812/79998.html

123 Mainstream media self-censorship http://rt.com/usa/mainstream-media-self-censorship-viewers-708/

124 The basal ganglia is located at the base of each hemisphere, and receives input from all four lobes, but have output only to the frontal cortex via the thalamus. Major activities include the planning of movement and all cognitive functions. Thought process disorders can result from disorders in the basal ganglia. Disorders of affect, cognition, Parkinson's, and Huntington's disease can result. Extra-pyramidal movements - involuntary movements such as tremors, rocking, and movement of limbs from psychotropic drugs stem from problems in the basal ganglia.

125 434 US 357 (1978), http://supreme.justia.com/cases/federal/us/434/357/case.html

126 US Supreme Court Delivers Blow to Fifth Amendment Right to Remain Silent During Police Questioning, Leaves Citizens With Burden of Knowing Rights June 17, 2013 https://www.rutherford.org/publications_resources/on_the_front_lines/us_supreme_court_delivers_blow_to_fifth_amendment_right_to_remain_silent_du

127 570 US _____ (2013)

128 30 US (5 Peters) 1 (1831)

129 Children of Incarcerated Parents: An Action Plan for Federal Policymakers, Council of State Governments Justice Center New York, New York, p. ix

130 Pogo - The comic strip philosopher.

CHAPTER 7

A VISIT FROM THE FBI

A wave of anger is sweeping the cities of the world. Politicians beware.[131]

About 10:00 a.m. one morning when I was having trouble getting out of bed, there was a loud knock on my door. I got up and went to the door and opened it. A man identified himself as an FBI agent and showed me his ID. He then asked if I knew why he was there. When I asked if it had anything to do with the challenge I had sent to the California Supreme Court, he turned 180 degrees and started to step away from the door before turning back to face me. "No," he said, "I'm here to investigate you for the Oklahoma City bombing."

After saying "You've got to be kidding," I excused myself to use the bathroom and also fix myself a cup of coffee. The agent refused the coffee I offered him, but we spent the next couple of hours, using the trunk of my car as a desk, talking, and providing copies of various documents, including the poorly written Supreme Court challenge that the court had rejected. By the time he left he seemed a little agitated at Senator Boxer, who had ordered the investigation as she didn't like a play I had written the evening following that bombing. No charges were filed against me.

The minor revisions I recently made to the play have more to do with formatting than content changes.

THE RIFLE
1995 (revised 2013)

SCENE I
SETTING: A kitchen in a modest home. On the wall, there is a rifle in a gun rack.
AT RISE: CONSTITUENT is muttering while typing. A beer is next to him on the table.
(For one minute the man types, muttering from time to time. He prints out what he has written, looks it over, puts the letter in an envelope, addresses the envelope, and then puts a stamp on it. He then takes a sip of the beer.)

SCENE II
SETTING: A congressperson's office.
AT RISE: Two women are standing near a desk.
(Congressional Intern MARY is reading CONSTITUENT's letter)
MARY: What should we do with this letter?
SUSAN (Mary's supervisor): Oh, ignore it; they all say the same thing.
MARY: Ignore it?
SUSAN: He can't expect us to take this seriously. He just needs to blow off some steam.

SCENE III
(Six months later)
SETTING: A kitchen in a modest home. On the wall, there is a rifle in a gun rack.
AT RISE: CONSTITUENT is muttering while typing. A beer is next to him on the table.
(Takes paper out of printer, reads it, smiles, puts letter in envelope, and fixes stamp to it.
He then takes rifle out of the gun rack and begins cleaning it.)

SCENE IV

SETTING: A congressperson's office.

AT RISE: Two women are standing near a desk.

MARY: Here's another letter from Citizen. What do we do now?

SUSAN: Ignore it.

MARY: Ignore it?

SUSAN: He hasn't any clout. He hasn't made any major campaign contributions. If it was really serious, he'd have his attorney write us. Obviously, he doesn't have much money, so he can't do anything for us. Ignore it. What can he do, blow up a building?

END PLAY

Following the various ordeals I endured in Los Angeles, I had written many letters, some of which could be considered angry letters to government officials. Most often the letters were ignored with no response ever received.[132] Some responses I received were to subjects other than what I had written about. On one occasion I did receive a sympathetic letter that directed me to a different agency. I had also been told by a half dozen attorneys that "it happens all the time, but there is nothing you can do about it," in reference to the actions of the police and public defenders.

I had left Los Angeles in 1994, shortly after both getting an attorney fired and having a short play produced at a small theater in Hollywood. After several months of living out of my car, camping out, and staying in cheap hotels and hostels, I moved into a small town in the eastern Sierras. There I volunteered at a fish hatchery and served on the county board of mental health, working on my recovery away from locations which triggered memories of abuse.

For three days following the FBI visit, I found myself shaking. My experiences in Los Angeles had left me wary of those in positions of authority. I was grateful that things had not gotten out of hand by the FBI visit, but at the time I was unaware of the value I had received. In nature, animals who escape attacks shake to dissipate the trauma before it lodges in their bodies. My shaking helped wash away the traumas I had experienced. My night sweats disappeared and I felt clean on the inside, although it would still be several years before I could speak of the various incidents without a huge lump coming to my throat and my eyes watering.

The visit from the FBI occurred several months after the bombing, when I was finishing a year of cognitive therapy, which is about learning better reactions to stress. At about the same time my doctors had decided I should no longer be considered disabled and began the process to end my disability benefits. While I had been considering moving to the San Francisco Bay area, I changed direction and moved to Nevada a few months later.

[131] The March of Protest, *The Economist* June 29, 2013

[132] The major exception was the response I received from Senator Ted Kennedy's office. I had sent the letter from the board and care I was living at, saying I could not believe what had been done to me. The kind response I received from the senator's office soothed me considerably.

CHAPTER 8

WHERE IS THE TOP OF A ROTATING SPHERE?
MORAL AUTHORITY IN THE TWENTY-FIRST CENTURY

*With slight shades of difference, you have the same religion,
manners, habits, and political principles. You have in a common
cause fought and triumphed together; the independence and
liberty you possess are the work of joint counsels, and joint
efforts of common dangers, sufferings, and successes.*[133]

Religious Strife in Early America

In Washington's time most were aware of the tyranny of state-sponsored religions. The emerging American nation had believers of various religious traditions. Most, although not all, were Christians of one stripe or another. Europe had known extreme religious persecution during the Inquisition, and the revocation of the Edict of Nates by King Louis XIV, a French monarch, in 1685 brought about a revival of religious intolerance that affected America as well as Europe.[134] Huguenots fled France, fearing death and imprisonment. Many found refuge in Holland and America, including the Dutch colony of New Amsterdam. In 1689, after William III, who had also been the stadtholder for the Dutch people, became king of England he urged passage of the Act of Toleration, although it did not go as far as he would have liked. It guaranteed religious toleration to certain Protestant nonconformists but still restricted the religious liberty of Roman Catholics, non-Trinitarians, and those of non-Christian faiths.[135] In Maryland, where many Catholics had emigrated to years earlier, they found they were no longer allowed to have any share in governing the colony and were encouraged to keep their religion to themselves.[136]

In July 1755, Charles Lawrence, British governor of Nova Scotia, ordered the mass arrests of Catholics in Acadia who refused to take an oath of allegiance to Britain, and many were relocated to various other colonies, including Massachusetts, Connecticut, New York, Pennsylvania, and North and South Carolina. Virginia refused the 1,100 exiles they were sent and shipped them to England where most then fled to France.[137]

The French crown's refusal to allow non-Catholics to settle in New France may help to explain that colony's slow rate of population growth compared to that of the neighboring British colonies, which opened settlement to religious dissenters. By the time of the French and Indian War (the North American front of the Seven Years' War), a sizeable population of Huguenot descent lived in the British colonies, and many participated in the British defeat of New France in 1759–1760.[138]

Washington and the other leaders of the American Revolution were well aware of the hatred and intolerance that could arise from religious mandates and were determined to prevent them from becoming ingrained in the new American nation. Many today seem to have forgotten this and appear to want to impose their religious beliefs on others.

Many of the nation's founders were deists, who, while believing in God, did not believe in the divinity of Christ, although they respected his teachings as good and wise. In this respect they were similar to the followers of Islam who also see Christ, like Muhammad as a holy person but human. Indeed this was the view of most Christians for the first three hundred to six hundred years of Christianity. Having Christ become the Son of God was little more than a marketing devise to make his teachings more acceptable to the Romans, who elevated sports heroes to god status, much as the media does today. It makes more sense that Christ was killed as the Pharisees (lawyer-priests who were later abolished) believed Pontius Pilate viewed him favorably and would install him and his followers as their replacements—middlemen between the Roman rulers and the people of Israel. Having a *jealous god* can make acts of violence inspired by jealousy acceptable.

President Eisenhower's Farewell Address

President Eisenhower, in his farewell address[139] stated, "Our people expect their President and the Congress to find essential agreement on issues of great moment, the wise resolution of which will better shape the future of the Nation." This is something that has been lacking for much of the last half century or so. For various reasons, many in America, including those in major cities, have become very parochial. They seem to know little of life outside their small circles. Much of the public no longer vote, seeing it as a waste of time. On most issues, the insular views of both major parties is overwhelming and outside the reality of a great many Americans. Imposing the views of their elites seems to be the major preoccupation of leaders in both houses of Congress.

At the time of President Eisenhower's farewell address, hope in America was riding high and pretty much everyone believed in the promise of a better future. Eisenhower did voice concerns, however:

> *This conjunction of an immense military establishment and a large arms industry is new in the American experience. The total influence-economic, political, even spiritual-is felt in every city, every state house, every office of the Federal government. We recognize the imperative need for this development. Yet we must not fail to comprehend its grave*

implications. Our toil, resources and livelihood are all involved; so is the very structure of our society.

In the councils of government, we must guard against the acquisition of unwarranted influence, whether sought or unsought, by the military-industrial complex. The potential for the disastrous rise of misplaced power exists and will persist.

We must never let the weight of this combination endanger our liberties or democratic processes. We should take nothing for granted only an alert and knowledgeable citizenry can compel the proper meshing of huge industrial and military machinery of defense with our peaceful methods and goals, so that security and liberty may prosper together.

The hope and excitement most had in the 1960s has been replaced by arrogance, contempt for the views of others, and pessimism. The halls of government rarely exhibit any statesmanship. Power brokers currently dominate. Money is the primary concern of most elected officials who apparently have a history of buying their way out of problems rather than working to solve them. For many, it seems that money is the sole path to happiness, and happiness is measured by how much control one has over others. Neither is the view of most Americans.

A June 2013 Gallup poll revealed that 70% of Americans hate their jobs or have "checked out" of them. Life may or may not suck any more than it did a generation ago, but our belief in "progress" has increased expectations that life should be more satisfying, resulting in mass disappointment. For many of us, society has become increasingly alienating, isolating and insane, and earning a buck means more degrees, compliance, ass-kissing, shit-eating, and inauthenticity. So, we want to rebel. However, many of us feel hopeless about the possibility of either our own escape from societal oppression or that political activism can create societal change.[140]

The Declaration of Independence states "that to secure these rights, Governments are instituted among Men, deriving their just powers from the consent of the governed,—That whenever any Form of Government becomes destructive of these ends, it is the Right of the People to alter or to abolish it, and to institute new Government, laying its foundation on such principles and organizing its powers in such form, as to them shall seem most likely to effect their Safety and Happiness."

The government of the United States is removed from the people. It is less just and operating without the consent of the people. Corporate megaliths appear to control all facets of government. Many people are beginning to raise their voices. Congress should listen and not just to those who can afford attorneys to circumvent the law. Both Republicans and Democrats seem interested primarily in tightening their respective party's grip, intent seemingly on destroying the principles America was founded upon.

Where Is the Top of a Rotating Sphere?

The huge increase in knowledge and abilities that have taken place in the last century or so—automobiles, airplanes, walks on the moon, deep-sea exploration, space stations, etc.— have led many to believe there will always be a technological fix to everything. This has caused many to discard any belief or concept of God. The petty view of God that some religious leaders demand is the only possible view of God has turned many away from religion as has the failure of religious leaders to overcome petty little differences, some appear to maintain that they have sole ownership of the *one true God*. For those who claim Christianity—or any religion—is superior to all others, a review of Adlerian psychology, which claims superiority is achieved by cooperating with others instead of competing with them, may be in order.

Life on planet Earth depends upon the sun, the planet rotating around the sun within certain parameters, and the moon revolving around the earth. When the sun, in some millions or billions of years, no longer keeps this planet within the Goldilocks zone or changes sufficiently in the light/heat it showers upon this wonderful globe, life will extinguish. There is an extremely small chance that, due to vents in the ocean floor, that some small forms of life could exist for hundreds or thousands of years more, but that is contingent upon volcanic forces still operating. The moon plays a part in the seasons as does the wobble around its axis that the earth has. We are all someplace on top of this of this rotating sphere. Why fight, kill, and otherwise harm others to show that *we* are on top?

Gratitude for Life

Gratitude for life itself should be the primary emotion we all have. We have the ability to thrive and overcome the obstacles we all face—without life we wouldn't have that opportunity. Religions have so far failed in their efforts to bring harmony to the people of the earth. They have, for the most part, been too busy demonstrating that they are superior to all other religions. Too much bickering over tiny little differences. All the religions have great teachings. Depending on time and circumstances, one teaching may be more appropriate for some people, while a different teaching is best for other people. A few months or years later, some other teaching may be more satisfying. Trying to impose one interpretation of any teaching is bound to cause more problems than it solves. People need to be free to decide for themselves. Often several meanings can be derived from one teaching. Economic gain for one group or another of people too often masquerades as religious dogma.

There are, of course, religious leaders who seek to have greater harmony among the various peoples of the earth. They understand that all religions have essentially the same or a similar message, just different messengers.

> *The great blessing from the Torah that's used by Jews and Christians alike is "The Lord bless you and keep you. The Lord make his face to shine upon you, and be gracious unto you. The Lord lift up his countenance upon you, and give you peace." (Numbers 6:22–26) . . . That's true in other religious traditions as well. Muslim doctrine and devotion speak of Ninety-nine Names of God. . . . the Friend, the Guide, the Guardian, the Advocate, the All-seeing, the Merciful, Beneficent, Compassionate, Patient, Gracious, Gentle(etc.)Just, Sublime, Wise, and Loving One. . . . The Hindu Mahabharata celebrates the Thousand Names of the Lord Vishnu, among them Creator, Giver of Peace, the All-Knowing, the Uplifter, the Lover, the Holder of the Wheel of the Cosmos, and the Protector.*[141]

God or nature—is there a difference? Some say yes, others say no. It's close to impossible to change the mind of anyone who has it closed. To some, God is nothing but a cruel hoax fostered upon people to perpetuate the rule of a greedy, uncaring elite. To some, God is outside the world and the universe—impossible to know. To others, God is the world and even more—and while it may be impossible for someone to know all of God, it is quite enjoyable to get to know God, even a little, as he (or she, if you prefer) is everywhere. Life is a gift; it can be found in the forest, in the desert, and in snails, fish, insects, trees, flowers, bears, rhinoceroses, everywhere and in whatever form. It is great to be human, to be able to use reason, to strive for understanding and harmony. Gratitude for life should be the norm. Yes, it can be difficult at times. Happy and content people don't seek to harm any, so teaching and allowing people to be happy is the best way to increase harmony in this world. Too many laws, regulations, and rules harm people needlessly. We are a diverse people, and we need to celebrate diversity. There are many ways to look at things and no one correct way. We need greater tolerance for the beliefs of all our various peoples.

Be Happy, Be Healthy, Be Peaceful, and Live in Harmony with Yourself and Others

The study of Buddhism has given me much contentment. It has eased my burden considerably so I can understand how others may view their religion in a similar way. Everyone should be allowed the opportunity to seek meaning in their lives without others imposing their views upon them. As not many Americans know much about Buddhism, I'll take a few moments to relate some of the teachings which are of significant to me.

Loving-Kindness Meditation
Metta Bhavana: The Cultivation of Universal Loving-kindness

May all beings be happy and peaceful.
(Free from suffering and distress)

May all beings be safe and secure.
(Free from fear and harm)

May all beings be healthy and prosperous.
(Free from pain, illness, and lack)

May all beings live joyfully and with ease.
(Free from struggle and conflict)

This meditation derives from the *Discourse on Loving-Kindness* (Metta Sutta) given by the Buddha 2,600 years ago. The loving-kindness he spoke of then is still the deepest need of the world today. The Pali word *metta* (*maitri* in Sanskrit) means universal loving-kindness, friendliness, and goodwill free from expectation and possessiveness. However, this is not the ordinary, sensual, emotional, or sentimental kind of love that most people commonly express. Metta is an all-embracing love—a sincere desire for the happiness and well-being of others. Metta is without any selectivity or exclusion. If we select a few people we love and exclude someone we do not like, this is a lack of understanding of metta. With a heart of love, we express care and concern for all beings through benevolent thoughts, feelings, and words, as well as through selfless acts of kindness and generosity.

The Four Noble Truths[142]

1. Truth of suffering (which declares that suffering exists).
2. Truth of cause of suffering (suffering is caused by the three poisons—ignorance, anger, and attachment).
3. Truth of the cessation of suffering (by overcoming the three poisons and realizing the true nature of mind, suffering will cease).
4. Truth of path (practicing wisdom and compassion is the [eightfold] path to become free from suffering).

The Eightfold Path

1. Right view
2. Right intention
3. Right speech
4. Right action
5. Right livelihood
6. Right effort
7. Right mindfulness
8. Right concentration

The eightfold path is simple, yet choosing what is right can be challenging at times.

Karma

No one else should be blamed for one's past history, present circumstances, or future happenings. The law of Karma is the ultimate form of personal responsibility.[143]

I greatly admired my father. He was able to do a difficult job under trying circumstances, and I never heard him complain. Several years after he was shot, I found out both the alleged shooter and the guy climbing over a fence, fleeing after an armed robbery, died in jail awaiting trial. My brother, the first officer on scene following the shooting, told me they had been beaten to death by fellow prisoners, but the way the story was told left me with doubts, but I lacked both the information and will to do anything about it. During my stays in the Los Angeles County jail, my thoughts would occasionally be of these two men. Whether or not karma had something to do with my being in jail, I cannot rule it out. Not wanting to die a meaningless death in jail, I proceeded on a journey, the destination of which is still unknown. "Hell in Buddhism is educative, not vengeful, and is not the sentence of a wrathful deity but the natural, unavoidable result of actions that violate dharma."[144] The journey is the reward.

The three poisons cause delusions which create negative karma, and this karma causes pain and unhappiness. On the other hand, positive mind and positive actions, including compassion and kindness, create a positive result, which is happiness and freedom from suffering.[145]

Justice in America

There is anger in America about the lack of justice. Courts are seen by many, especially those on the lower rungs of the economic spectrum, to be nothing more than a total farce designed to keep some people perpetually down while enforcing rules of a belligerent, uncaring wealthy population that subsides on the misery of millions. This is perhaps most evident in our drug laws. In Buddhism, anger is seen as clouding the mind, and righteous anger—although coming from a source of injustice—is not seen as a solution. Instead, calm, mindful action is seen as the appropriate antidote to injustice.

> *Between 1980 and 2013, the number of incarcerated federal drug defendants soared from 4,749 to 100,026— an astonishing 2,006 percent. As of September 28, 2013, half—50.1 percent—of all federal prisoners were serving time for drug offenses. In fiscal year 2012 alone, 26,560 men and women were convicted of federal drug crimes.*[146]

These drug laws are nonsensical. There are various reasons people use drugs. Some try them to see for themselves if what they have heard—about them being so bad or so good—is true or not. A few try them, hoping they will have some sort of religious experience. Most use them as a way to avoid pain. Often it is past traumas that people are trying to overcome, which is the source of the pain they are trying to escape. Many become addicted and are unable to stop using the drugs. Criminalizing behavior that is partially out of the individual's control is not good policy. Imprisoning people without ever letting them have their say, as is all too common in the America of today, is also bad policy. Even though drug usage is not a path that will bring greater happiness to individuals, the disincentives imposed have done little to nothing to reduce drug usage. This can be proved out, in part, by one of the fundamentals of economics—people respond to incentives while disincentives do nothing to promote certain activities.

It will probably never be proven one way or another to the satisfaction of all, but there is evidence that some of the drug laws were promoted into existence by former FBI Director J. Edgar Hoover as part of a blackmail payment. Hoover claimed for many years that there was no such thing as organized crime, despite substantial evidence and proof that the mafia did exist and exerted control over substantial amount of crime in the nation. Was the mafia blackmailing him? Was promoting illegality of drugs partly a scheme to increase profits of organized crime and was just blackmail for keeping Hoover being a transvestite secret? While some evidence exists, it is not conclusive. Those in government will likely never be persuaded he was, for it would tarnish the image of everyone in government always being squeaky clean. It is, however, a source of humor for those who are anti-authoritarian, and humor is good for the soul, whether one believes in a soul or not.

Can the United States regain the moral authority this nation had in the peak years from the end of the World War II to the mid-1960s?

Some on Wall Street seem to have mistaken their huge egos for the source of all life. While they may be free to worship their own behinds, they should not expect others to join the choir and sing their praise. At this time, however, it appears that much of Congress, as well as many in the executive branch, as well as a majority of the Supreme Court have acted in a manner to compel Americans to consider Wall Street the supreme deity. Hopefully Amendment I—"Congress shall make no law respecting an establishment of religion, or prohibiting the free exercise thereof; or abridging the freedom of speech, or of the press; or the right of the people peaceably to assemble, and to petition the Government for a redress of grievances"—will stand despite efforts by some so-called liberal Democrats to change it.

At the current time, there is a divide between the political Left and Right. Difficult questions, often involving life, liberty, and the pursuit of happiness, are at the core of some differences. Often both sides appear to advance one argument for their position while denying that same argument for the other side. The right wing is generally opposed to laws and court decisions that permit abortion and various means of birth control. They advance the argument that the possible life of an unborn trumps the right of women to have the liberty to prevent or terminate a pregnancy. They appear willing to prevent a woman from pursuing her happiness to force the birth of an unwanted child. They appear willing to prevent women from becoming full citizens. The left wing generally states that this is an area that should totally be up to the individual woman involved as it is her body. Neither man nor woman is the property of the government, even if part of the Left seems willing to have a bureaucracy impose its collective beliefs on everyone else.

There is another moral position that must be considered. It has to do with the growing world population and the fact that an increased population means increased starvation, wars, uncertainty over availability of scarce resources, and decreased standard of living for many. Why should women be forced to bring children into an increasingly dangerous world? Wouldn't it make more sense to work for greater peace and prosperity for all who inhabit the world?

Another divide between Left and Right is the question of rights for homosexuals. Some on the Right have extremely harsh views taken from some religious texts on how those who are attracted to members of the same sex should be treated. Yet evidence[147] exists that various manufactured chemicals have entered the waters of America and of the world, which have contributed to an increased prevalence not just of mental disorders, as presented in the first chapter, but of homosexuality as well. Could this merely be God or nature's way of saying lack of adequate planetary stewardship has consequences?

Can America—and the World—Meet These and Other Challenges?

Can America and the world meet these and other challenges, or will we prove unwilling to rationally address the many ways we have slipped from pursing ideals?

As I see it, the human race has three options:

A. Increase respect for individual liberty while working for harmony between individuals, nations, and the natural world.
B. Seek revenge and domination for past injuries, real or imagined.
C. Slip into confusion and inaction not knowing how to proceed.

I hope we can choose wisely.

Organizing people has never been my strong suit, but I believe people must organize to end the scapegoating and other abuses fostered on the American people, particularly those who have been labeled as mentally ill.

Recommendations

1. The Koran algorithm should be used regularly at emergency rooms when people are brought in for evaluations and before anyone is committed to a psychiatric hospital or is sent to prison. Ideally the Koran algorithm (see appendix) should be performed by general practitioners every three to five years beginning around puberty and continuing to middle age when the onset of mental health problems begins to wane. Perhaps it should again be periodically performed when individuals enter their senior years.

2. Trauma screening should be part of every mental health examination and be included in annual checkups done by general practitioners. This way, patients can be referred to one or more of the proven nondrug therapies and avoid being labeled as mentally ill, which can condemn an individual to a substandard life. (Symptoms for trauma are nearly the same as for most *mental illnesses*—both major and minor.)

3. Magnesium levels should be checked routinely in the mental health system, as well as in prisons and youth correctional facilities. Ideally they should also be done by general practitioners. (*"Magnesium is essential in regulating central nervous system excitability thus magnesium deficiency may cause aggressive behavior, depression, or suicide. Magnesium calms the brain and people do not need to become severely deficient in magnesium for the brain to become hyperactive . . . a marginal magnesium intake overexcites the brain's neurons and results in less coherence—creating cacophony rather than symphony—according to electroencephalogram (EEG) measurements."*[148])

4. Protest various Supreme Court decisions (*Miranda v. Arizona, Imbler v. Pachtman, Bordenkircher v. Hayes, Frazier v. Cupp, Salinas v. Texas*) have resulted in this nation, either inadvertently or not, becoming totalitarian—essentially eliminating the right to fair and speedy trials while basically eliminating the right of the accused to speak in court. This has resulted in increased crime and widespread contempt of the justice system, not to mention the millions of unjustly imprisoned people.

5. Write letters to elected representatives.

6. Organize protests in front of the Supreme Court, jails, prisons, courts, and mental health facilities. Perhaps Bastille Day, July 14, and days during May, which is Mental Health Month, and during October, which is

Mental Illness Awareness Month, would be the best for organizers of these events.

7. File lawsuits in the appropriate state, local, and federal courts.

8. Vote for candidates who support rights for individuals over increased bureaucratic and corporate rights.

9. Work to make your community a better place to live and bring joy to the downtrodden.

"Whenever the roles of individuals within a group become specialized, it becomes both possible and easy for the individual to pass the moral buck to some other part of the group. In this way, not only does the individual forsake his conscience but the conscience of the group as a whole can become so fragmented and diluted as to be nonexistent... The plain fact of the matter is that any group will remain inevitably potentially conscienceless and evil until such time as each and every individual holds himself or herself directly responsible for the behavior of the whole group –the organism-of which he or she is a part" [149]

133 Washington's Farewell Address, 1796; http://www.gpo.gov/fdsys/pkg/ GPO-CDOC-106sdoc21/pdf/GPO-CDOC-106sdoc21.pdf

134 The Birth of A Nation 1968 by Arthur M. Schlesinger p. 8

135 http://en.wikipedia.org/wiki/William_III_of_England

136 Men, Women and Manners of Colonial Times, Vol.II by Geo. Fisher 1913, p. 216

137 Great Events from History, The 18th Century Vol 1 1701–1774 Edited by John Powell, Oklahoma Baptist University, Salem Press 2006, p. 383

138 http://en.wikipedia.org/wiki/French_and_Indian_War

139 See http://www.ourdocuments.gov/doc.php?flash=true&doc=90&pag e=transcript for the complete 1961 speech

140 The US is experiencing an epidemic of crippling mental illness. Is it life in the United States that is driving people to depression and stress? By Bruce E. Levine, www.alternet.org August 4th, 2013 http://www.alternet.org/ personal-health/whats-behind-dramatic-rise-mental-illness

141 Excerpt from THE FACES OF GOD, A Sermon by Dean Scotty McLennan, University Public Worship Stanford Memorial Church May 19, 2013

142 Ancient Teachings in Modern Times, Buddhism in the 21st Century by the Venerable Lama Losang Samten, p. 44

143 RIVER OF FIRE RIVER OF WATER (pp. 158–159)

144 The Dhammapada Introduced and translated by Eknath Easwaran 1985, 2007 p. 215- dharma is defined as "the central law of life, that all things and events are part of an indivisible whole, p. 20.

145 Ancient Teachings in Modern Times, p. 43

146 An Offer You Can't Refuse, How US Federal Prosecutors Force Drug Defendants to Plead Guilty, p. 17 Human Rights Watch

147 Environmental causes of homosexuality http://www.viewzone2. com/phthalates.html / Chemical Pollution Linked to Upsurge in Homosexuality Transgenderism http://www.worldissues360.com/ index.php/chemical-pollution-linked-to-upsurge-in-homosexuality-transgenderism-3906/

148 *Transdermal Magnesium Therapy* (2007) by Mark Sircus, Ac., OMD, p. 5

149 *People of the Lie; The Hope for Healing Human Evil* by M. Scott Peck, MD (pg. 218)

APPENDIX

Union of Concerned Scientists

Citizens and Scientists for Environmental Solutions

Industry Influence on Drug and Medical Device Safety at FDA
$700 million in lobbying buys significant access
March 29, 2012

2012 is crucial for the Food and Drug Administration, as Congress votes on legislation to renew the Prescription Drug User Fee Act (PDUFA) and the Medical Device User Fee Act (MDUFA). Every five years, Congress by law must approve negotiations between the FDA and industries it regulates that set the fees these companies pay to the agency. In return, the companies exact performance goals from the FDA aimed at reducing the time it takes to get a drug or device approved.

It is crucial that Congress makes sure that safety, not industry profits, remains the FDA's priority, and that the agency is able to use the best available scientific information to do its job. However, several legislative proposals now before Congress would increase industry influence over FDA and make the agency's scientists more vulnerable to political and corporate pressure. A new analysis by the Center for Responsive Politics commissioned by the Union of Concerned Scientists (UCS) suggests that hundreds of millions of lobbying dollars, combined with millions in targeted campaign contributions, are helping to shape these congressional proposals.

THE CONTEXT FOR THIS ANALYSIS In 2007, the last time PDUFA and MDUFA came before Congress, the FDA had been shaken by serious scandals and drug recalls. FDA whistleblowers testified at congressional hearings that the FDA attempted to suppress and intimidate them when they raised serious concerns about the safety of specific drugs later found dangerous and withdrawn from the market.

These scandals paved the way for real reform. That year, the PDUFA law greatly increased the transparency of the drug approval process and curbed conflicts-of-interest at the agency. It also strengthened the role of FDA scientists, requiring the agency to respect and encourage their right to publish in peer-reviewed journals and stipulating that the views of dissenting drug reviewers were to be part of the public record when a drug was approved by the agency.

But the political climate has changed. Congress, far from building on the reforms of 2007, seems eager to roll them back and pass legislation that reads like an industry gift list: relaxing FDA's review standards, particularly for medical devices; rolling back needed financial conflict-of-interest rules; and even changing the mission of the FDA to include job creation.

In part, this new direction reflects a change in political priorities in Congress. The unemployment picture has led many members of Congress of both parties to attack regulations and regulatory frameworks they have long despised, falsely believing that their actions will create jobs. But is another factor the role of special interest money on Capitol Hill? 2

MEASURING SPECIAL INTEREST INFLUENCE UCS asked the Center for Responsive Politics for data on lobbying expenditures and political contributions for three industries: pharmaceutical companies; medical device companies, and biotechnology firms for the three-year period beginning

January 1, 2009 and ending December 31, 2011. Among the top findings:

Lobbying
From 2009 through the end of 2011, prescription drug, biotechnology and medical device companies and their trade associations spent more than $700 million lobbying Congress and the Administration. Drug companies and their associations alone spent more than $487 million. Biotechnology and medical device companies and their associations also made significant investments, spending $126 million and $86 million on lobbying respectively. Here is the spending by all three industries broken down by year:

These industries, of course, lobbied on a variety of issues pending before Congress and the Executive Branch (such as the Affordable Care Act). Since registered lobbyists and their clients do not have to report the specific issues on which they lobbied, there is no way to break down how much money was spent to lobby on PDUFA and MDUFA. That said, money builds relationships and buys access, and we know that PDUFA and MDUFA are critical to each of these special interests.

By comparison, in the same time frame, the oil and gas industry spent more than $467 million on lobbying, while electric utilities and the insurance industry each spent more than $480 million, according to the Center for Responsive Politics:

Political Contributions
The prescription drug, biotechnology, and medical device industries were generous with campaign contributions to members of Congress, targeting nearly $6.3 million to the campaign and political action committees of 70 lawmakers who served on key legislative committees overseeing drug and medical device safety legislation from 2009 through 2011.

Two congressional committees do the heavy lifting on PDUFA and MDUFA: the House Energy and Commerce Committee's Subcommittee on Health, currently with 25 members, and the Senate Health Education Labor and Pensions Committee (HELP), currently with 21 members.

During the 2009–2010 two-year election cycle, these industries gave more than $4.4 million to members of the House health subcommittee and the Senate HELP committee. In 2011, the first year of the 2011–2012 election cycle, these same interests gave more than $1.8 million to members of these two key committees:

Drug, device, and biotechnology companies and their trade associations give to both Republicans and Democrats:

LEGISLATIVE CHALLENGES TO FDA'S SCOPE AND AUTHORITY The power of these special interests is reflected in the number of industry-friendly bipartisan legislative proposals pending before both the House and the Senate. Various proposals would:

- Add job creation to the FDA mission, diluting the agency's focus on protecting the public from unsafe medical products and bringing safe products to market.
- Reduce the scrutiny the agency could give to medical devices by compelling the agency to consider every "least burdensome" alternative to improving device safety.
- Impose more bureaucratic hurdles on the resource-strapped agency.
- Erode the FDA's standard of "substantial evidence" when reviewing drugs and devices, overturning a crucial scientific element of the Food, Drug, and Cosmetics Act.

Some in Congress also want to give companies more influence over the FDA scientific advisory committees that evaluate the safety and effectiveness of prescription drugs by relaxing financial conflict-of-interest standards for these committees. 6

Representatives of the Pharmaceutical Research and Manufacturers of America (PhRMA) and the Biotechnology

Industry Organization (BIO) criticized the current process for vetting advisory panel members for financial ties to the industries with products under review by a panel. David Wheadon, senior vice president for regulatory affairs for PhRMA, questioned the need for screening for conflicts in the first place, contending that industry expertise should not be considered a "penalty" by the FDA.

BIO representative Richard Pops went even further. In his testimony, Pops charged: "In recent years, arbitrary limits and unnecessarily restrictive interpretations of conflict of interest rules have created barriers that have prevented FDA from consistently recruiting highly qualified scientific advisors."

FDA Commissioner Margaret Hamburg paints a different picture. In testimony before Congress this year, she made clear these strengthened conflict-of-interest standards were not creating problems for the agency, while admitting the agency faced some challenges in finding enough experts for some of its advisory panels. Commissioner Hamburg told Congress that the agency had experienced no problems keeping the number of waivers it issues within the limit set by current law.ii

PROGRESS ON CONFLICTS-OF-INTEREST MADE IN RECENT YEARS

Conflicts-of-interest and their influence on FDA science long has been a concern to medical experts. The Institute of Medicine, in an exhaustive report on conflicts in medical research, science and education, observed that "*concerns are growing that wide-ranging financial ties to industry may unduly influence professional judgments involving the primary interests and goals of medicine. Such conflicts-of-interest threaten the integrity of scientific investigations, the objectivity of professional education, the quality of patient care, and the public's trust in medicine.iii*

In 2006, the concern about financial conflicts was shared by a bipartisan group in Congress. Republican Senators Michael Enzi and Chuck Grassley both raised questions about conflicted experts in the FDA approval process. Concluding an investigation of the role of certain plastic surgeons with ties to implant makers on an advisory panel that in 2005 recommended the reentry of silicone breast implants into the market, Sen. Enzi remarked, "We will build on the findings of this investigation by including provisions to address the problem of potential conflicts of interest among advisory committee members in the drug safety bill Sen. Edward Kennedy (D-Mass.) and I are preparing for introduction." [i]

In 2007, Congress approved the Food and Drug Administration Amendments Act (FDAAA), which strengthened conflict-of-interest provisions at the agency. Iv The law required FDA to:

- Reduce the number of waivers it granted to conflicted experts by 5 percent over each of 5 years. This reduction covered the number of conflicted experts in the aggregate.
- Tell the public when the agency granted a waiver that allowed a conflicted expert to serve on a committee. The law required the FDA to publish the name of the expert and specific information about the nature of the conflict on the agency's website.
- Be more aggressive in recruiting non-conflicted experts.

i   Hearing on Prescription Drug User Fee Act Reauthorization before House Energy and Commerce Subcommittee on Health, Political Transcript Wire, 3 Feb. 2012.

ii   Anna Yukhananov, "No need to loosen conflict rules, U.S. FDA head says," Reuters, 1 February 2012.

iii "Conflict of Interest in Medical Research, Education and Practice, Institute of Medicine, Washington: The National Academies Press, 2009, 1.

[i] http://www.fdanews.com/newsletter/article?issueId=6334&articleId=61354

iv   Erin D. Williams and Susan Thaul, "FDA Amendments Act of 2007 (P. L. 110–85)," Congressional Research Service, April 27, 2010, 61.

Many believe that Congress should ban conflicts-of-interest outright. Ideally, individuals with expertise that panels needed who have conflicts-of-interest would be permitted only to present before a committee and answer questions, and would be precluded from voting to approve or deny a drug or medical device application. Because human lives are at stake, conflicted experts should not be able to inappropriately influence advisory committee decisions.

Transforming Diagnosis
By Thomas Insel, Director, NIMH
April 29, 2013

In a few weeks, the American Psychiatric Association will release its new edition of the *Diagnostic and Statistical Manual of Mental Disorders* (*DSM-V*). This volume will tweak several current diagnostic categories, from autism spectrum disorders to mood disorders. While many of these changes have been contentious, the final product involves mostly modest alterations of the previous edition, based on new insights emerging from research since 1990 when *DSM-IV* was published. Sometimes this research recommended new categories (e.g., mood dysregulation disorder) or that previous categories could be dropped (e.g., Asperger's syndrome).

The goal of this new manual, as with all previous editions, is to provide a common language for describing psychopathology. While *DSM* has been described as a "Bible" for the field, it is, at best, a dictionary, creating a set of labels and defining each. The strength of each of the editions of *DSM* has been "reliability"— each edition has ensured that clinicians use the same terms in the same ways. The weakness is its lack of validity. Unlike our definitions of ischemic heart disease, lymphoma, or AIDS, the *DSM* diagnoses are based on a consensus about clusters of clinical symptoms, not any objective laboratory measure. In the rest of medicine, this would be equivalent to creating diagnostic systems based on the nature of chest pain or the quality of fever. Indeed, symptom-based diagnosis, once common in other areas of medicine, has been largely replaced in the past half century as we have understood that symptoms alone rarely indicate the best choice of treatment.

Patients with mental disorders deserve better. NIMH has launched the Research Domain Criteria (RDoC) project to transform diagnosis by incorporating genetics, imaging, cognitive science, and other levels of information to lay the foundation for a new classification system. Through a series of workshops over the past 18 months, we have tried to define several major categories for a new nosology (see below). This approach began with several assumptions:

- A diagnostic approach based on the biology as well as the symptoms must not be constrained by the current *DSM* categories,
- Mental disorders are biological disorders involving brain circuits that implicate specific domains of cognition, emotion, or behavior,
- Each level of analysis needs to be understood across a dimension of function,
- Mapping the cognitive, circuit, and genetic aspects of mental disorders will yield new and better targets for treatment.

It became immediately clear that we cannot design a system based on biomarkers or cognitive performance because we lack the data. In this sense, RDoC is a framework for collecting the data needed for a new nosology. But it is critical to realize that we cannot succeed if we use *DSM* categories as the "gold standard." The diagnostic system has to be based on the emerging research data, not on the current symptom-based categories. Imagine deciding that EKGs were not useful because many patients with chest pain did not have EKG changes. That is what we have been doing for decades when we reject a biomarker because it does not detect a *DSM* category. We need to begin collecting the genetic, imaging, physiologic, and cognitive data to see how all the data— not just the symptoms—cluster and how these clusters relate to treatment response.

That is why NIMH will be reorienting its research away from *DSM* categories. Going forward, we will be supporting research projects that look across current categories—or subdivide current categories—to begin to develop a better system. What does this mean for applicants? Clinical trials might study all patients in a mood clinic rather than those meeting strict major depressive disorder criteria. Studies of biomarkers for "depression" might begin by looking across many disorders with anhedonia or emotional appraisal bias or psychomotor retardation to understand the circuitry underlying these symptoms. What does this mean for patients? We are committed to new and better treatments, but we feel this will only happen by developing a more precise diagnostic system. The best reason to develop RDoC is to seek better outcomes.

RDoC, for now, is a research framework, not a clinical tool. This is a decade-long project that is just beginning. Many NIMH researchers, already stressed by budget cuts and tough competition for research funding, will not welcome this change. Some will see RDoC as an academic exercise divorced from clinical practice. But patients and families should welcome this change as a first step towards "precision medicine," the movement that has transformed cancer diagnosis and treatment. RDoC is nothing less than a plan to transform clinical practice by bringing a new generation of research to inform how we diagnose and treat mental disorders. As two eminent psychiatric geneticists recently concluded, "At the end of the 19th century, it was logical to use a simple diagnostic approach that offered reasonable prognostic validity. At the beginning of the 21st century, we must set our sights higher."

(http://www.nimh.nih.gov/about/director/2013/transforming-diagnosis.shtml)

A Medical Algorithm for Detecting

Reprinted with permission from Hospital and Community Psychiatry, December 1989 Vol. 40 No.12 (Copyright ©1989) American Psychiatric Association

Physical Disease in Psychiatric Patients

Harold C. Sox Jr., M.D.
Lorrin M. Koran, M.D.
Carol H. Sox, M.S.
Keith I. Marton, M.D.
Fred Dugger, P.A.
Teruko Smith, R.N.

An algorithm for screening psychiatric patients for physical disease was empirically derived from a comprehensive assessment of 509 patients in California's mental health system. The first 343 patients were used to develop the algorithm, and the remaining 166 were used as a test group. Calculations were made for several versions of the algorithm, and the data were compared with the diagnoses listed in the patients' admission mental health records. The algorithmic procedure was more accurate and more cost-effective than the medical evaluation procedures used by the state mental health system. When applied to the test group, the algorithm detected up to 90 percent of patients who had an active, important physical disease at a cost of $156 per patient. The mental health system had detected 58 percent of test-group patients with a disease at a cost of $230 per patient.

Many mental health programs are not staffed with physicians practiced in medical diagnosis and thus are unprepared to detect a large proportion of physical diseases in their patients.

As described elsewhere, California's state mental health system programs fail to detect many diseases that could be causing or exacerbating psychiatric disorders (1). Mental health programs need effective methods for screening their patients for physical disease.

Ideally, the methods should be suitable for use by personnel with little medical training. A number of articles have discussed the detection of physical illness in patients with mental disorders (2-9). Most have described the frequency of physical diseases in the patients, and some have suggested strategies for screening. A medical algorithm, which is a set of instructions for solving a clinical problem (10,11), is one screening strategy especially well suited to personnel with little medical training. In this paper, we describe the development and testing of an algorithm that uses the patient's history and blood pressure and selected diagnostic tests to detect physical disease in persons with mental disorders. The algorithm, which is based on a comprehensive clinical evaluation of patients drawn from public sector mental health programs in California, detected more diseases at a lower cost per diagnosed case. A preliminary report of our findings has appeared in abstract form (12).

Other screening studies

Several other studies have addressed the best way to screen for physical disease in mentally ill persons. Hall and associates (2,3) evaluated acutely ill psychiatric inpatients with a comprehensive battery of procedures that was more thorough and costly than ours ($400 in 1979 dollars). They found that patients with more than four symptoms had a particularly high incidence of serious disease. Three other studies, each in narrowly defined patient populations, suggested that a small amount of data will detect most physical disease. In a sample of chronically ill outpatients, Barnes and associates (4) found that a fasting serum glucose, urinalysis, blood pressure, and a careful review of systems disclosed 75 percent of diagnoses that were new or required treatment. Eastwood and Tennent (5) found that measuring blood pressure and performing blood hemoglobin and urinalysis would have detected 75 percent of disease in psychiatric patients seen in an emergency room. Dolan and Mushlin (6) found that 4 percent of psychiatric inpatients had important medical diseases that could be reliably diagnosed by a battery of ten laboratory tests. In contrast to the earlier studies, we studied patients from across the spectrum of public mental health programs. We also present several alternative versions of the screening algorithm and assess the tradeoffs between detection rates and costs.

Methods

Our study subjects were 509 patients in 25 of California's county-operated mental health programs and one state hospital. We performed a standardized evaluation that included a complete history obtained through a questionnaire, a physical examination, and laboratory screening tests. Study internists reviewed the data and referred patients whose results suggested previously undiagnosed disease to community internists or neurologists. The study internists then reviewed all data, including any reports from community physicians, and made a final diagnosis. It was assumed that the internists detected all causes of active physical illness, and thus their diagnosis became the "gold standard" for the presence of disease in patients who had been referred to them.

Some patients had an active, important physical disease, as defined by one of five criteria: the disease was acutely life threatening, could cause or exacerbate a psychiatric disorder, was communicable, had potentially significant long-term health consequences, or was chronic and could markedly impair self-esteem by causing disfigurement, social stigma, or loss of role functioning. Using recursive partitioning, we identified the best predictors of these diseases and combined them into clinical algorithms for disease detection. The process of enrolling patients, obtaining data, and establishing the diagnosis of active, important disease has been described elsewhere (1).

Formulating the screening algorithm. Our goal was to develop a screening procedure that could be used by mental health program personnel with limited physical assessment skills. Therefore, we used only the history questionnaire findings, the laboratory test panel results, and the vital signs (blood pressure, pulse, and temperature) as clinical predictors of disease. After all final diagnoses had been assigned, the algorithm was developed on the first 343 study patients (the training set).

We used recursive partitioning to identify the best combination of findings for detecting active physical disease (13). As applied to medical diagnosis, recursive partitioning is a cyclic procedure for subdividing a population into groups that have different prevalences of active physical disease. The process requires a computer file that contains a standard set of data, including a final diagnosis, on each of many patients. The first step of each cycle identifies the clinical finding that best discriminates between patients with the disease and patients without the disease. The second step of each cycle divides the population into two groups: patients with the highly discriminatory findings and patients without it. In the group in which none of the members have the finding, the prevalence of disease is relatively low. In the second cycle, the process is repeated for both of the subgroups created in the first cycle. Thus at the end of the second cycle there are four subgroups. The process may be repeated for many cycles, until no additional discriminatory findings are identified.

For classifying a patient, each clinical finding can be regarded as a fork or node in an algorithm, with one fork to be followed when the finding is present and another when it is not present. To use a recursive partitioning algorithm, a health worker obtains the clinical finding specified by the first fork, follows the appropriate branch to the next fork, and obtains the clinical finding specified there. The process is repeated until there are no more branches. The prevalence of disease in the subgroup at the terminal fork is used as an estimate of the probability of disease in the patient.

We modified the recursive partition process slightly. In each cycle, we partitioned only the group with the lower likelihood of disease. The criterion for deciding whether a finding increased the likelihood of active disease was its likelihood ratio- its frequency in patients with an active disease by its frequency in patients with no active disease. In the first cycle of our recursive partitioning process, clinical findings with a likelihood ratio of at least 10 were identified (see nodeA of Figure 1). All patients with one or more of these findings were removed from the training set. The second cycle was performed on the patients remaining in the training set. We identified findings with a likelihood ratio of at least 5.5 (node B of Figure 1) and again removed patients with one or more of these findings from the training set. This process was repeated six times, with progressively lower likelihood ratios, at which point running additional cycles did not identify more patients with a physical disease. **Evaluation of the screening algorithm.** We used the screening algorithm to classify the remaining 166 patients (the test set) and compared the accuracy of classification for test-set patients with that for the training- set patients. We used two measures to evaluate the accuracy of each node. One was the number of patients with an active disease who were classified as having active disease by the node and all preceding nodes. We expressed this measure as the cumulative proportion of diseased patients that the algorithm had identified as likely to be diseased (the true-positive rate, or sensitivity). The other measure was the cumulative proportion of nondiseased patients that the algorithm had identified as likely to be diseased (the false-positive rate). We compared the algorithm's accuracy for the training set with that for the test set by plotting the cumulative true-positive and false-positive rate values as two receiver-operating characteristic (ROC) curves, one for the training set and one for the test set (14,15) (figure 2).

Costs of evaluating patients for physical disease. The legislation authorizing this study required that we estimate the cost-effectiveness of physical disease screening as currently performed by state- and county- operated mental health programs in California. To establish the cost of screening, we reviewed each patient's mental health file and itemized all medical evaluation procedures and tests listed in the administration workup of study patients (performed in the first 72 hours of hospitalization or the first two visits to an outpatient setting).

This method may underestimate the true cost because physicians' return visits in inpatient settings were not recorded, and we could not include the $33 Medicaid payment for return visits. We used Medicaid payment rates, obtained from the state Medicaid data system, as a proxy for the costs of screening by the county mental health programs. We did not include health costs billed to Medicare or third-party insurance, costs paid directly by the patient, and non-collectible costs because they were not of interest to the [sentence incomplete in original].

We measured the cost of the screening protocol performed on all study patients and estimated the cost

Figure 1
Algorithm for detecting active physical disease in psychiatric patients

Explanation of Figure 1

The algorithm depicted in Fig places a patient in one and only or group. To obtain the odds that a p has active physical disease, multip odds of physical disease in the pa mental health program (see Tabl the odds of disease in the differen tal health programs in this study) likelihood ratio (L.R.) enclosed box corresponding to the patient group.

Example: Suppose that a day tre: patient has none of the findings in l node A but has a history of se (branch node B). The prevalence ease for patients in day treatmen (the corresponding odds are .39 The odds of disease for this patie the product of the prior odds (.3! and the likelihood ratio for a po finding at branch node B (5.7). Th of disease are therefore 2.22 to 1, corresponds to a .69 probability of disease. If the same patient has n the findings at any of the branch no through F, the odds of disease wo the product of the prior odds (.3! and the likelihood ratio if no findir present (.21), or .08 to 1. Th responding probability of active c is .07, as given by the formula prob = odds/(1 v + odds).

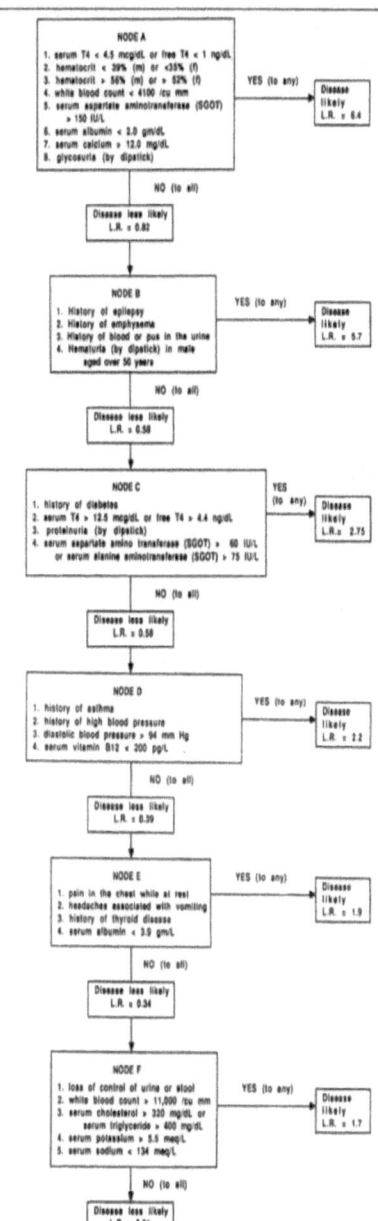

of using the algorithm. We assumed that the examination would be performed in a state or county program whose costs would be paid directly by public funds. Therefore, we estimated the total cost of the examinations from the salaries of the physician's assistants that reflected the time spent on this part of the project, and the Medicaid payment for the services provided by the community physician to whom we referred patients for a definitive evaluation. The cost per patient of the tests used for the screening protocol were urinalysis (by dipstick), $2.24; chemistry panel, $14.75; complete blood count, $5.53; total serum thyroxine and 3,5,3' –triiodothyronine (T3) uptake, $11.17; blood drawing, $5.85; and serum B12, $16.57. The cost of the entire panel of diagnostic tests, including tests that were not used for this algorithm in Figure 1, was $83.31, which included handling costs and the salaries of the study internists who reviewed data to decide whether the patient should be referred for further evaluation. The cost for obtaining a complete medical history was estimated at $13.84; the $.07 oer history question was rounded up to $.10 for calculating the cost of using the screening algorithm. The total for the physical examination was $18.60, including $1.95 for taking blood pressure. The cost to Medicaid of referring patients to an internist was $32.95; the average charged by the community physicians was $82.77.

We defined the cost-effectiveness of the screening methods as the cost per case of active, important disease detected, which was calculated by dividing the total cost of screening all patients by the number of patients with newly detected disease. The marginal cost-effectiveness of an additional step in the screening algorithm was the incremental cost of obtaining the additional data divided by the number of diseased patients identified by the additional step. The unit cost of screening – cost per patient screening – was the total cost divided by the number of patients screened. In calculating cost-effectiveness, we assumed that every patient referred for definitive evaluation would keep the appointment with the physician. In fact, missed appointments are common, and recontacting the patient incurs additional program costs.

Results

Detection of physical disease by the mental health system.
A detailed report of the characteristics of the study population
and the detection of physical disease by the California mental
health system has been published elsewhere (1). The principal
finding of the study reported in that paper was the prevalence
of undiscovered physical disease. Of the 509 patients, 200 (39
percent) had at least one active physical disease. The specific
disease categories are listed in Table 1. The screening program
discovered a previously undiagnosed active, important disease in
63 patients (12 percent). The county mental health program was
aware of only 47 percent of the 291 active, important diseases.

Table 3
Prevalence of active physical disease in mental health programs

Program category	N pa-tients	Prevalence of active disease	Odds of active disease
Crisis intervention	53	.43	.75:1
Psychiatric inpatient			
(24-hour acute hospital)	63	.44	.79:1
Psychiatric health facility			
(24-hour acute nonhospital)	55	.36	.56:1
Outpatient	136	.42	.72:1
Day treatment (partial care)	58	.28	.39:1
Skilled nursing facility	51	.26	.35:1
Community board-and-care home	40	.33	.49:1
State hospital	53	.57	1.33:1

Detecting physical disease. The purpose of the screening algorithm is to identify which patients should be referred from the mental health program to a physician. As shown in Figure 1, when any of the findings at a branch node were present, the patient was placed in a subgroup that was at relatively high risk of having a physical disease.

There are several versions of the algorithm. One may choose to obtain the data for the first branch node (Algorithm A), for all six branch points (Algorithm F), or for an intermediate number of branch nodes (Algorithms B through E). Depending on which version of the algorithm is used, up to 93 percent of training-set patients and 90 percent of test-set patients with active, important disease were correctly placed in one of the high-risk categories (Table 2). The screening algorithm identified a much greater proportion of the patients with active, important physical disease than did the state and county mental health programs. The medical record used by the mental health

Detecting physical disease. The purpose of the screening algorithm is to identify which patients should be referred from the mental health program to a physician. As shown in Figure 1, when any of the findings at a branch node were present, the patient was placed in a subgroup that was at relatively high risk of having a physical disease.

Table 1
Active, important physical diseases identified by study assessment in 509 mental health program patients[1]

Disease	N[2]
Cardiovascular	48
Eye	2
Gastrointestinal	39
Gynecological	2
Hematological	23
Metabolic and endocrine	37
Musculoskeletal	3
Neurologic	81
Respiratory	28
Skin	20
Toxic	2
Urological and renal	5
Miscellaneous	2

[1] Source: Koran and associates (1)

programs contained a notation of important disease in only 49 percent of the training-set patients and 59 percent of the test-set patients who had active, important disease.

The performance of all versions of the algorithm in the test-set population was similar to that in the training-set population, as shown in the receiver-operating characteristic (ROC) curve in Figure 2. Each of the six versions of the algorithm is represented on the ROC curve by a point whose location is determined by its true-positive and false-positive rates. The ROC curve representing the test set is slightly below the training set curve, indicating that all versions of the algorithm detect physical disease in a new patient population nearly as accurately as in the population for which they were designed. The versions that required more data (Algorithms E and F) identified more diseased patients than versions that required less data (Algorithms A and B). However, the versions that detected most of the diseased patients also classified many patients who did not have active disease as at relatively high risk for having active disease.

The screening algorithm was also

used to calculate the odds of a patient's having active, important physical disease. According to Bayes' theorem, the odds of disease after the disclosure of a new finding equals the product of the odds of disease before disclosure and the likelihood ratio for the finding. Thus when a patient had any of the findings at a branch node, the odds of finding physical disease increased by an amount proportional to the likelihood ratio for the node (see boxes to the right of the nodes in Figure 1). When all findings at a node were absent, the odds of finding physical dis-

ease decreased by an amount proportional to the likelihood ratio (see boxes below the nodes in Figure 1).

To calculate the odds that a patient had an active, important physical disease, one uses the patient's clinical findings and the screening algorithm to place the patient in a subgroup. The odds that the patient has an active disease is the product of the likelihood ratio of the patient's subgroup and the odds of disease before screening. The odds of disease before screening must be obtained from the overall prevalence of physical disease in the type of mental health program in which the patient is enrolled. Mental health program staff must either measure the prevalence of active physical disease in their program or use as a proxy the prevalence in the programs that we studied (Table 3).

Cost-effectiveness of screening methods. The screening algorithms were more cost-effective than the medical evaluation procedures of the state and county mental health programs. We measured the cost-effectiveness of the algorithms in two ways. First, we calculated the total cost of using the screening algorithm as the sum of the direct cost of the screening procedures and the cost of referring the study's high-risk patients to a physician (Table 4). However, the costs incurred when patients were referred by the county mental health programs were not known because we did not know the number of patients who had a referral visit.

Therefore, to compare the

screening algorithm to the screening procedures of the mental health programs, we calculated the cost of using the algorithm without including referral costs (Table 2). The cost per patient screened ($59 with Algorithms E and F) was similar to that of the mental health system ($57). The cost per patient with active physical disease was $174 for Algorithm E and $156 for Algorithm F, compared with $231 for the mental health programs' procedures. The complete evaluation that we performed on all study patients cost $116 per patient and $274 per patient with active, important disease.

Screening for physical disease resulted in some patients' being referred for further testing to determine whether disease was present. The total cost of screening includes these additional costs (Table 4). The total cost per patient with active disease was $232 for Algorithm E and $216 for Algorithm F. Table 4 also shows the marginal cost-effectiveness (additional cost per additional case detected) of including more clinical findings as indications for referral.

Discussion

The principal finding of our study of disease detection by state and county mental health programs was the need for improved screening for physical disease. We found that 12 percent of the patients had important physical disease that was not known to either the patients or the mental health system. We have identified screening strategies that were effective in our study population yet were relatively inexpensive.

In developing a systematic strategy for screening, one could use the clinical judgment of an individual or a consensus of several clinicians. Alternatively, one could perform a prospective study of patients, as we did. This report could be used to guide the design of a prospective study, or a program could adopt one of the algorithms that we developed.

These algorithms have been studied carefully in our representative population but their accuracy may be different in another patient population (5).

Our algorithms provide a choice of screening strategies. How should one choose a strategy? One approach is to maximize the probability that a patient referred for definitive diagnosis will be found to have physical disease. This approach is efficient but risky. The algorithm used might contain only the first two branch nodes (Algorithm B). Even if none of the findings at nodes A and B were present, the probability of disease would still be quite high. Alternatively, one could choose an algorithm that detects as many diseased patients as possible. To do so, one must use an algorithm that has many branch nodes (Algorithms E or F). This approach is safe but costly

because the algorithm requires a relatively large quantity of data and because its false-positive rate is relatively high. Still another approach might be to use the ROC curve shown in Figure 2 and analytic methods for choosing the optimal operating point on the curve (14,15). Finally, many clinicians will choose the algorithm that detects as many diseased patients as possible within the constraints of the program budget. Tables 2 and 4 contain the information needed to predict the program cost of each algorithm. A clinical laboratory can help to reduce costs by producing a panel of tests that contains only the tests required by the chosen version of the algorithm.

....

The algorithms would have detected far more diseased patients than the state mental health system but would have failed to detect a small number of diseased patients who would have been identified had each patient received a full history, physical examination, and diagnostic test panel. Health professionals who administer screening programs must

remain alert to the possibility that patients who have a negative screening result may still have disease. Such patients may be incorrectly reassured and may fail to seek medical advice despite symptoms of disease. The probability of a false-negative result is much lower in an outpatient setting, where the overall prevalence of disease is low, than in an inpatient setting such as a state mental hospital.

In this study, we began the process of validating our algorithm by applying it to a new population (the test set) and measuring its true-positive and false-positive rates, which should be the same in all populations. Because the study team moved from site to site, later patients were from different clinical settings than were the earlier patients. As shown in the ROC curve in Figure 2, all algorithms performed similarly in the training and test populations. The next step in validation is a study by different investigators in a different clinical setting. Ideally, investigators at each site where an algorithm is used should perform a

validation study with their patients, using the same methods as the investigators who developed the algorithm.

This study has several potential shortcomings. First, we enrolled only 54 percent of the patients that we invited to participate. Many nonenrolled patients were more outwardly hostile and appeared more violent than enrollees. The practical effect of this selection bias may not be large, as such patients may not cooperate with any screening efforts. Second, because we referred only half of the patients for a definitive clinical evaluation, we may have missed some serious diseases that our algorithm is not designed to detect. However, we do not think that much significant illness was missed. When the screening procedures were repeated on 90 of the nonreferred patients, only one patient had an important disease that we failed to identify at the time of the initial screening evaluation (hyponatremia). Third, because the training set contained relatively few patients who received any single diagnosis, the algorithms may miss patients with atypical findings of these diseases. Fourth, we may have underestimated the total cost of screening because we did not measure screening program costs induced by discovering disease. The follow-up period was too short to make meaningful measurements of the costs of treatment or mental health care costs that might have been averted by treatment of physical disease.

Our screening procedures can be performed by mental health program personnel with little or no additional training. They can identify many more diseased patients than current screening procedures, at about the same cost per patient screened. This systematic approach could improve the results achieved by the mental health care system.

Figure 2; Tables 2 and 4 not included in permission to reprint

Acknowledgments

The authors thank Connie Gibney for collecting the data on patients' evaluation by the mental health programs and Satish Chandra, M.D., Kent Imai, M.D., Thomas G. Kelsy, M.D., Larry C. Levin, M.D., S. Allen Dorosin, M.D., Edward R. Hatton, M.D., Jerrod Normanly, M.D., Ljudevit Andres, M.D., Pablo Romero, M.D., and Theodore Rose, M.D., for evaluating study patients. The research was supported by California Department of Mental Health contract 82-73099 A-1.

References

1. Koran LM, Sox HC, Marton KI, et al: Medical evaluation of psychiatric patients: results in a state mental health system. Archives of General Psychiatry 46:733–740, 1989

2. Hall RCW, Popkin MK, Devalu RA, et al: Physical illness presenting as psychiatric disease. Archives of General Psychiatry 35:1315–1320, 1978

3. Hall RCW, Gardner ER, Stickeny SK, et al: Physical illness manifesting as psychiatric disease, II: analysis of a state hospital inpatient population. Archives of General Psychiatry 37:989–995, 1980

4. Barnes RF, Mason JC, Greer C, et al: Medical illness in chronic psychiatric outpatients. General Hospital Pyschiatry 5:191–195, 1983

5. Eastwood MR, Mindham RHS, Tennent TG: The physical status of psychiatric emergencies. British Journal of Psychiatry 116:545–550, 1970

6. Dolan JG, Mushlin AI: Routine laboratory testing for medical disorders in psychiatric inpatients. Archives of Internal Medicine 145:2085–2088, 1985

7. Roca RP, Breakey WR, Fischer PJ: Medical care of chronic psychiatric outpatients. Hospital and Community Psychiatry 38:741–745, 1987

8. Ferguson B, Dudleston K: Detection of physical disorder in newly admitted psychiatric patients. Acta Psychiatrica Scandinavica 74:485–489, 1986

9. Colgan J, Philpot M: The routine use of investigations in elderly psychiatric patients. Age and Aging 14:163–167, 1985

10. Sox HC, Sox CH, Tompkins RK: The training of physician's assistants: the use of a clinical algorithm system for patient care, audit of performance, and education. New England Journal of Medicine 288:818–824, 1973

11. Komaroff AL, Black WL, Flatley M, et al: Protocols for physician assistants: management of diabetes and hypertension. New England Journal of Medicine 290:307–312, 1974

12. Koran LM, Sox HC, Sox CH, et al: Detecting disease in psychiatric patients (abst). Medical Care 12S:S99, 1987

13. Wasson JH, Sox HC, Neff RK, et al: Clinical prediction rules: applications and methodologic standards. New England Journal of Medicine 313:793–799, 1985

14. McNeil JB, Keller E, Adelstein SJ: Primer on certain elements of medical decision making. New England Journal of Medicine 293:211–215, 1975

15. Metz CE: Basic principles of ROC analysis. Seminars in Nuclear Medicine 4:283–298, 1978

SCHOPENHAUER'S THIRTY-EIGHT (UNETHICAL) WAYS TO WIN AN ARGUMENT

Arthur Schopenhauer (1788–1860) was a brilliant German philosopher. These thirty-eight stratagems are excerpts from *The Art of Controversy*, first translated into English and published in 1896.

Schopenhauer's thirty-eight unethical ways to win an argument are as follows:

1. Carry your opponent's proposition beyond its natural limits; exaggerate it. The more general your opponent's statement becomes, the more objections you can find against it. The more restricted and narrow his or her propositions remain, the easier they are to defend by him or her.

2. Use different meanings of your opponent's words to refute his or her argument.

3. Ignore your opponent's proposition, which was intended to refer to a particular thing. Rather, understand it in some quite different sense, and then refute it. Attack something different than that which was asserted.

4. Hide your conclusion from your opponent till the end. Mingle your premises here and there in your talk. Get your opponent to agree to them in no definite order. By this circuitous route you conceal your game until you have obtained all the admissions that are necessary to reach your goal.

5. Use your opponent's beliefs against him. If the opponent refuses to accept your premises, use his own premises to your advantage.

6. Another plan is to confuse the issue by changing your opponent's words or what he or she seeks to prove.

7. State your proposition and show the truth of it by asking the opponent many questions. By asking many wide-reaching questions at once, you may hide what you want to get admitted. Then you quickly propound the argument resulting from the opponent's admissions.

8. Make your opponent angry. An angry person is less capable of using judgment or perceiving where his or her advantage lies.

9. Use your opponent's answers to your questions to reach different or even opposite conclusions.

10. If your opponent answers all your questions negatively and refuses to grant any points, ask him or her to concede the opposite of your premises. This may confuse the opponent as to which point you actually seek them to concede.

11. If the opponent grants you the truth of some of your premises, refrain from asking him or her to agree to your conclusion. Later, introduce your conclusion as a settled and admitted fact. Your opponent may come to believe that your conclusion was admitted.

12. If the argument turns upon general ideas with no particular names, you must use language or a metaphor that is favorable in your proposition.

13. To make your opponent accept a proposition, you must give him or her an opposite, counter-proposition as well. If the contrast is glaring, the opponent will accept your proposition to avoid being paradoxical.

14. Try to bluff your opponent. If he or she has answered several of your questions without the answers turning out in favor of your conclusion, advance your conclusion triumphantly, even if it does not follow. If your opponent is shy or stupid, and you yourself possess a great deal of impudence and a good voice, the trick may easily succeed.

15. If you wish to advance a proposition that is difficult to prove, put it aside for the moment. Instead, submit for your opponent's acceptance or rejection some true proposition, as though you wished to draw your proof from it. Should the opponent reject it because he or she suspects a trick, you can obtain your triumph by showing how absurd the opponent is to reject a true proposition.

Should the opponent accept it, you now have reason on your own for the moment. You can either try to prove your original proposition or maintain that your original proposition is proved by what the opponent accepted. For this, an extreme degree of impudence is required.

16. When your opponent puts forth a proposition, find it inconsistent with his or her other statements, beliefs, actions, or lack of action.

17. If your opponent presses you with a counter proof, you will often be able to save yourself by advancing some subtle distinction. Try to find a second meaning or an ambiguous sense for your opponent's idea.

18. If your opponent has taken up a line of argument that will end in your defeat, you must not allow him or her to carry it to its conclusion. Interrupt the dispute, break it off altogether, or lead the opponent to a different subject.

19. Should your opponent expressly challenge you to produce any objection to some definite point in his or her argument, and you have nothing much to say, try to make the argument less specific.

20. If your opponent has admitted to all or most of your premises, do not ask him or her directly to accept your conclusion. Rather draw the conclusion yourself as if it too had been admitted.

21. When your opponent uses an argument that is superficial, refute it by setting forth its superficial character. But it is better to meet the opponent with a counter argument that is just as superficial, and so dispose of him or her. For it is with victory that you are concerned, and not with truth.

22. If your opponent asks you to admit something from which the point in dispute will immediately follow, you must refuse to do so, declaring that it begs the question.

23. Contradiction and contention irritate a person into exaggerating his or her statements. By contradicting your opponent you may drive him or her into extending

the statement beyond its natural limit. When you then contradict the exaggerated form of it, you look as though you had refuted the original statement your opponent tries to extend your own statement further than you intended, redefine your statement's limits.

24. This trick consists in stating a false syllogism. Your opponent makes a proposition and by false inference and distortion of his or her ideas you force from the proposition other propositions that are not intended and that appear absurd. It then appears the opponent's proposition gave rise to these inconsistencies, and so appears to be indirectly refuted.

25. If your opponent is making a generalization, find an instance to the contrary. Only one valid contradiction is needed to overthrow the opponent's proposition.

26. A brilliant move is to turn the tables and use your opponent's arguments against him or herself.

27. Should your opponent surprise you by becoming particularly angry at an argument, you must urge it with all the more zeal. Not only will this make the opponent angry, it may be presumed that you put your finger on the weak side of his or her case, and that the opponent is more open to attack on this point than you expected.

28. This trick is chiefly practicable in a dispute if there is an audience who is not an expert on the subject. You make an invalid objection to your opponent who seems to be defeated in the eyes of the audience. This strategy is particularly effective if your objection makes the opponent look ridiculous or if the audience laughs. If the opponent must make a long, complicated explanation to correct you, the audience will not be disposed to listen.

29. If you find that you are being beaten, you can create a diversion that is, you can suddenly begin to talk of something else, as though it had bearing on the matter in dispose. This may be done without presumption if the diversion has some general bearing on the matter.

30. Make an appeal to authority rather than reason. If your opponent respects an authority or an expert, quote that authority to further your case. If needed, quote what the authority said in some other sense or circumstance. Authorities that your opponent fails to understand are those which he or she generally admires the most. You may also, should it be necessary, not only twist your authorities, but actually falsify them, or quote something that you have invented entirely yourself.

31. If you know that you have no reply to an argument that your opponent advances, you may, by a fine stroke of irony, declare yourself to be an incompetent judge.

32. A quick way of getting rid of an opponent's assertion, or throwing suspicion on it, is by putting it into some odious category.

33. You admit your opponent's premises but deny the conclusion.

34. When you state a question or an argument, and your opponent gives you no direct answer, or evades it with a counter question, or tries to change the subject, it is a sure sign you have touched a weak spot, sometimes without knowing it. You have as it were, reduced the opponent to silence. You must, therefore, urge the point all the more, and not let your opponent evade it, even when you do not know where the weakness that you have hit upon really lies.

35. This trick makes all unnecessary if it works. Instead of working on an opponent's intellect, work on his or her motive. If you succeed in making your opponent's opinion, should it prove true, seem distinctly to his or her own interest, the opponent will drop it like a hot potato.

36. You may also puzzle and bewilder your opponent by mere bombast. If the opponent is weak or does not wish to appear as if he or she has no idea what you are talking about, you can easily impose upon him or her

some argument that sounds very deep or learned, or that sounds indisputable.

37. Should your opponent be in the right but, luckily for you, choose a faulty proof, you can easily refute it and then claim that you have refuted the whole position. This is the way which bad advocates lose a good case. If no accurate proof occurs to the opponent or the bystanders, you have won the day.

38. A last trick is to become personal, insulting and rude as soon as you perceive that your opponent has the upper hand. In becoming personal you leave the subject altogether, and turn your attack on the person by remarks of an offensive and spiteful character. This is a very popular trick, because everyone is able to carry it into effect.